MOUNTAIN HIGH

Roy Bedford

Original Watercolour Paintings by Roy Bedford

A mountain shows many faces, and many moods.
Blistering heatwaves,
Wind, rain and snow,
The dark of night, when the moors belong to
the wild things that move, and screech, and fly.

Good Walking

Roy

Published by *WAKEWALKER* Books
23 Manor Rise, Walton, Wakefield WF2 6PF
Telephone (0924) 257065

© Text by Roy Bedford 1994
© Original Watercolour Paintings by Roy Bedford 1994
© Cover Design by Roy Bedford 1994

ISBN 0 9522261 1 1

British Library Cataloguing-in-Publication Data.
A catalogue record for this book is available from the British Library.

Typesetting with the invaluable assistance of
Yorkshire Art Circus, Castleford

Printed by FM Repro, Repro House, 69 Lumb Lane
Roberttown, Liversedge, West Yorkshire WF15 7NB

All rights reserved. No part of this publication may be reproduced, stored in a retrieval system, or transmitted, in any form or by any means, electronic, mechanical, photocopying, recording or otherwise without prior permission of the Copyright owner.

CONTENTS

In Trouble Again   7

Helvelyn   17

Blencathra   20

Helm Crag   33

The Cobbler   35

Mardale   38

Buttermere   49

The Heatwave   53

Holme Moss   57

Robinson   62

Snowdon   65

The Rakes   69

Eagle Crag   73

Barf   77

Great Gable   80

Reflections   83

ILLUSTRATIONS

Original Watercolour Paintings by Roy Bedford

Cover picture — The Langdale Valley

Striding Edge, Helvelyn	9
Blencathra and the Stone Circle	10
Helm Crag from Grasmere	11
Helm Crag, the Lion and the Lamb	12
The Cobbler, Scotland	13
Buttermere from High Stile	14
Elter Water	15
Waterhead, Ambleside	16
Holme Moss	25
Borrowdale slate quarries	26
Hindscarth from Newlands	27
Scafell Pike and Scafell	28
Grange Bridge	29
Pavey Ark - Jack's Rake	30
Loughrigg Tarn	31
Eagle Crag	32
Haweswater	41
Mardale - lost village	41
Snowdon	42
The Bridge House, Ambleside	43
The Ridge, Hindscarth	44
Stonethwaite	45
Barf	46
The Bishop	46
Great Gable	47
Stockley Bridge	48

THE LAKE DISTRICT

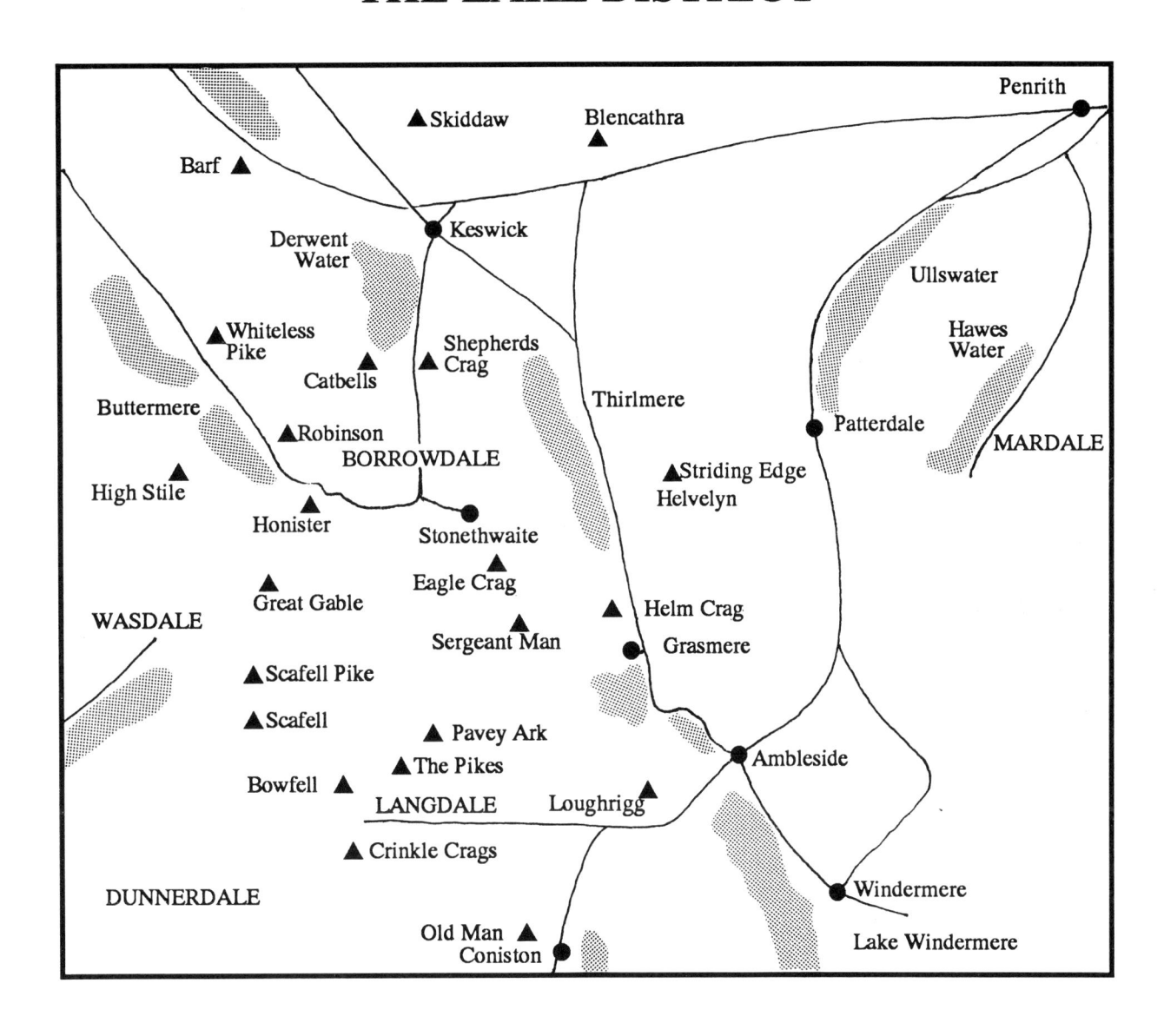

Thanks

to the many friends and colleagues,
organisations and clubs,
whose valuable assistance and expertise
contibuted greatly towards this publication

especially

The Yorkshire Art Circus,

In Trouble Again

The mountain tops disappeared again in a swirl of cloud.

"There's no sign of a break," Dave announced, creeping back into the shelter. "Turning to sleet again!"

It wasn't much of a shelter, just a crack in the rocks, where a large flat one leaned against the crags. There was only just enough room for Roy and Dave to huddle inside. At least they were protected from the worst effects of the rain, although the cold wind still whistled through, making their wet anoraks and trousers feel like cold bathwater.

"Where's the tribe?" Roy enquired. "Can you see them?"

"No, I think they found a cave, just below that overhang. They'll be all right."

"Still got eight of them?"

"Think so... There were eight when we set off, and I don't think we've lost any."

The boys were all from a local school. The oldest was fifteen, the youngest only eleven. There was no real cause for concern. They were all capable of looking after themselves, and this November expedition into the hills shouldn't have posed any great problems for them.

The snow underfoot was wet and slushy. It might easily have melted away, but the icy wind and persistent sleet showers had lowered the temperature again, and snowflakes were beginning to spin round in the lee of the crags.

Lunchtime was greeted with loud cheers from the boys, and they lost no time finding shelter amongst the rocks which made up the summit of the fell, leaving Roy and Dave to eat their sandwiches in peace.

"Oh, hell, salmon paste again!"

"I thought you liked salmon."

"Not this sort. It's got ice in it."

The tomatoes were no better, old, dark red, skins as tough as leather.

"I'll go and see if Brian's got any chicken left.... and offer him one of these tomatoes."

Roy had just started to ease himself out of the shelter when Peter came running up towards him, laughing all over his face.

"Clive's lost his boot!"

Roy looked at Peter with some amusement. "Lost his boot? Where?"

"Over there.... see that stream, and the boggy bit where the cows have churned it up."

"Yes."

"It's in there. Can't find it!"

"How did he manage that?"

"He got stuck. We were chasing him for his cap, and we all went through the mud. That's when he lost it."

Roy couldn't hold back the grin.

"Then you'd better find it!"

Peter was just about to go, when a sorry-looking figure appeared by his side. It was Clive. He was a walking advertisement for mud. There was mud everywhere, plastered on his trousers, his shirt, on his face, his hands, and down the front of his anorak. It even dripped off his elbow as he held onto his cap.

His one remaining boot was hardly recognisable as such. A disgusting liquid sludge ran down his leg, over his sock, inside the boot-top, and oozed out through the lace-holes. On his other foot was something which must have been a sock, half on and half off, caked with pure moorland slime in shades of black, brown and yellow.

"Lost me boot, sir!"

"I can see that. What are you going to do now?"

"Find it."

"So?"

"Brian's looking for it."

"Then you'll all have to look for it, won't you?"

"Yes, sir."

In Trouble Again

The pair of them galloped down the hillside to the stream, where two of their mates had already begun to turn the ground over with some pieces of wood.

"Give them half an hour," Dave suggested. "It'll keep them busy!"

Roy managed to move some flat stones to make a rough seat, and they settled down with cups of steaming coffee.

"Good old Clive," Dave laughed. "Not a bad kid, but when anything happens, it's always him!"

"Yeah, bad luck seems to follow him around."

"Reminds me of those youth courses we did in Keswick."

"And Wales," added Roy. "We had a few heart attacks on that one!"

Dave finished his coffee, and began to pack his rucksack again.

"You know, we had some good walks in those days," he said. "Did you finish that book you were writing?"

"You mean...."

"Yes, when you nearly broke your neck on Honister Crag."

"Ahh, that one! Yes, I got it finished. You should go and buy one."

"Maybe... What else is in it?"

"All sorts," Roy replied. "Winter camping, then we did Coniston Old Man... got caught in a thunderstorm and then it snowed."

"You did Scafell?"

"Yes, and Ben Nevis. That was wild. Incredible place!"

"OK, you've convinced me. I'll go and buy one next week."

Dave began to move out of the shelter. It was time they were heading for home.

"Don't forget Clive," Roy reminded him. "If we don't find his boot, we'll have to carry him down."

"Or leave him."

"Can we do that?"

MY MOUNTAINS, the ideal complement to this book, is available from many bookshops.

Within its gripping chapters, Roy takes us through the joys and trials of expedition, often in adverse weather conditions, on many of the popular mountain routes of England, Scotland and Wales.

The book contains graphic descriptions of memorable climbs, and the conditions which made them so unusual.

He introduces the reader to the techniques of rock climbing, and recalls the special humour of youth expeditions. Oh, those incorrigible kids!

The author has again illustrated the book with a collection of original watercolour paintings.

MY MOUNTAINS   Published by *WAKEWALKER* Books in January 1994

Helvelyn

Striding Edge and Helvelyn

featured in a following chapter, page 17

Reproductions from water colour originals
by Roy Bedford ©

Blencathra

Blencathra, and the Castlerigg Stone Circle

featured in a following chapter, page 20

Reproductions from water colour originals
by Roy Bedford ©

Helm Crag

Helm Crag, from Grasmere village

featured in a following chapter, page 33

Reproductions from water colour originals
by Roy Bedford ©

Helm Crag

Helm Crag, the summit formation, known as the Lion and the Lamb

featured in a following chapter, page 33

Reproductions from water colour originals
by Roy Bedford ©

Scotland

Ben Arthur, The Cobbler, Scotland *featured in a following chapter, page 35*

Buttermere

*Buttermere Valley
from the High Stile ridge*

featured in a following chapter, page 49

Reproductions from water colour originals
by Roy Bedford ©

Elter Water

Elter Water

between Ambleside and the Langdales

Reproductions from water colour originals
by Roy Bedford ©

Ambleside

Waterhead, Ambleside
Loughrigg in the background

Loughrigg is featured in a following chapter,
page 53

Reproductions from water colour originals
by Roy Bedford ©

Helvelyn

"Striding Edge!" Roy announced.

Jeff looked a little apprehensive.

"Are you sure you know what you're doing?"

"Piece of cake!" Roy retorted. "We'll have it cracked by lunchtime."

Jeff wasn't entirely convinced, but decided he wasn't going to let the opportunity pass him by, and fell in behind Roy and his huge rucksack before they disappeared into the trees.

Striding Edge is perhaps the most favoured of all the routes onto Helvelyn from Patterdale. It is a name which conjours up an impression of dizzy heights and knife-edge traverses, a ridge with a reputation. To many a seasoned walker it represents an opportunity to enjoy the exhilaration of the finest ridge walk in the Lake District.

Roy and Jeff, working colleagues in an industrial setting, had planned this route for some weeks over cups of coffee in the canteen. Like many workers, they found the office routines just too cumbersome, too little opportunity to get out and enjoy their outdoor interests. It was with great joy, therefore, that they embarked on their summer holiday, setting up camp near Ullswater and arriving in Patterdale on a breezy but fine Monday morning, ready for anything!

The first stage of the climb was a pleasant incline through woods onto the shoulder of a small ridge overlooking the lake. Nestling in the trees on the hillside they discovered Lanty's Tarn, a gem of a pool, set between green banks, with superb views over the valley.

The morning sun slanted through the trees, lighting up the ripples over the surface of the Tarn. It was a scene of tranquility, rivalling that of Ullswater itself.

"Just the spot for coffee," Jeff suggested.

"Already? Are you feeling well?"

Jeff nodded. It was probably no more than an excuse to stop.

Soon they spotted a wooden stile on the crest of the ridge, about a mile ahead. "Half-way point," Roy explained.

It seemed an eternity before they reached the sharp scramble leading up to it. The incline had been relentless, not steep or difficult, but continuous, with the stile acting like a carrot to a donkey, drawing them like a beacon.

"Looks like everyone stops here," Jeff remarked. "The grafiti!"

Chalked on the woodwork of the stile were various messages such as "Bob, gone up, see you there." There were, of course, the usual carvings, but no sign of Kilroy, though it's a level bet he'd already been there.

The main message, however, was "700 yards to journey's end," in big white letters.

It really did seem like journey's end. The hard slog was behind them, and just over the cluster of rocks ahead they saw the tip of Helvelyn. Patchy white cloud wafted across the summit, coming and going with each turn of the wind. It seemed that, with reasonable luck, it would remain clear enough for them to see some extensive views from the top.

Jeff led the way round a rocky outcrop, and suddenly stopped in his tracks. "Hell, look at that!"

Striding Edge was only fifty yards away. The chain of narrow crags stood like dinosaur teeth, prehistoric battlements on a knife-edged ridge. It was a daunting proposition, three hundred yards of dizzy scrambling which they would have to negotiate if they were to reach the summit.

They stood for a while, looking at it, alarmed by the way it fell away steeply on both sides, into the heads of two valleys, Grisedale and Red Tarn.

It was at this point that they noticed something very odd, which made them reach for the cameras.

Helvelyn

On the Grisedale side, cloud billowed upwards in a turbulent grey mass. Then as it rose, the wind caught it, pulling it back into the valley.

The black, jagged teeth of the Edge stood in relief against the white backcloth of rising cloud, looking like the rim of a volcano. If anyone was in any doubts about the reputation of Striding Edge, then surely this was the confirmation.

Remarkably, the right hand side of the ridge was completely clear of cloud.

As Roy and Jeff watched, they noticed that several more walkers had caught up, and having seen the unusual spectacle, took out their cameras and recorded the scene for the benefit of their colleagues back home.

Roy turned to Jeff. "OK, who's first?"

Taking out his own camera, he motioned Jeff onto the ridge, and took a couple of photographs as Jeff positioned himself on the first pinnacle.

It was easy going at this point, as the rocks were flat, and any bumps in the path had been worn off by years of use. The pinnacles ahead, however, were a different proposition. They looked positively rough, dangerous and dramatic.

Jeff, meanwhile, was playing at "now you see me, now you don't," standing with his left foot in cloud, and his right one in bright sunshine. Dodging to the left, he almost disappeared. One pace to the right and he was clearly visible, jumping up and down with excitement.

Then he realised that he had to be very careful. Too much open space!

Red Tarn seemed close, lying in the basin below the Edge. The placid surface reflected the blue sky and fleecy clouds scudding overhead. The water was so clear it was easy to see submerged rocks below the surface.

It seemed from where he stood, that Jeff could drop straight into the water from his lofty perch, and as if to prove the point, he tossed a stone towards the tarn.

He was surprised to see that he couldn't throw it far enough to get anywhere near the water. He threw another rock, and watched it soar through the air for an interminable time, finally clattering on the scree far below, well short of the tarn. How deceptive distances can be.

Roy put away the camera, and as he caught up he found Jeff examining a plaque which had been erected on the Edge itself, commemorating the tragic loss of a member of the local hunt.

"This is definitely John Peel country," Jeff remarked.

"Yes, but what was he doing up here?" asked Roy.

Their guide book confirmed that it was the Dixon Memorial, and this unfortunate man appears to have fallen whilst hunting foxes. It was still beyond credibility that foxes should venture onto Striding Edge, but there was the proof, believe it or not!

They began to progress onto the second pinnacle. The friendly level track suddenly became a rough, narrow edge, little wider than the sole of a boot. It was dry enough to be fairly safe, although the effect on the mind was dramatic, conjouring up fears of disappearing into the valley.

Gusts of wind made the going hazardous at times, and Roy sank to his knees during a particularly fierce blast.

He paused to admire the view of Grisedale, now visible like an aerial map stretched out below him.

"The cloud's gone!" he exclaimed.

"Yeah.... I got that funny feeling," Jeff remarked, "like I had on Blackpool Tower."

Continuing along the Edge, they saw that there were two alternative paths for much of the way. One rugged track clung to the crest of the pinnacles, whilst the other was a dirty brown path just below the line of the crags, where the hillside dropped away towards Red Tarn.

Using the ridge path wherever they could, they made good progress until eventually the way was lost in a confusion of rocky outcrops. Even the easy alternative track had disappeared.

The problem arose at a point where a deep cleft sliced into the ridge, and they had to descend some fifteen feet from the pinnacle.

Roy eased himself slowly down the rocks, swinging on good handholds, and reaching down with a boot to find a ledge lower down. Not a place to juggle with a camera!

"It's OK," he called. "Take your time."

Jeff followed carefully. How could he possibly go wrong?

Helvelyn

There were obviously two ways of tackling a descent like this, forwards or backwards. He tried going forwards, but the handholds were a bit sparse, the heels tended to slip, and the rucksack got in the way. Not good for the ego!

Then he tried it backwards. Yes, this presented better handholds, and the toe-holds were easier to find. However, it was very difficult to see where he was going.

With renewed confidence he proceeded to lower himself from ledge to ledge. He was doing well, until suddenly he couldn't find the next ledge with his right foot.

"Help, I'm stuck!"

His left boot was still at shoulder height, wedged in the toe-hold which had been so safe and secure - so secure he couldn't get it out. He was in the splits position and hadn't the strength to go up again.

Roy went back to help. It took several good blows with his hand to dislodge the jammed boot, and Jeff was able to continue, looking more embarrassed than hurt.

There was more excitement as another party came into view. It was a family group, with two teenagers and a Jack Russell terrier. "What's a dog doing on a walk like this?" thought Roy.

The poor animal hadn't a chance. The woman had carried it most of the way, but the awkward descent into the gully was proving impossible for them. Roy climbed up to try and help. "OK - throw him down!"

Straddling between two rocks, he was able to reach up for the terrier and pass it down to the outstretched arms of Jeff, standing below. The woman, too, needed help to negotiate the descent. Her legs were just not long enough. But all ended well, and they disappeared along the edge towards Helvelyn. They would obviously find another way down for their return.

Suddenly the end of the ridge appeared, almost as an anticlimax. The path from the last pinnacle rose into a jumble of broken rocks, and continued upwards onto the contours of Helvelyn.

It was desperate scrambling in places, difficult to stay upright on the loose rubble which filled every groove and crevice. The effects of erosion had made the track very hazardous.

The reward for all the hard work was a final grassy ascent onto the summit plateau. They had made the top!

They paused for a few moments regaining their breath. Striding Edge looked impressive from above, but somehow not as dramatic as that first sighting from the lower ridge. Walkers could be seen strung out along its length, picking their way over the pinnacles. Their progress appeared just as slow as Roy and Jeff's had been. This ridge was truly a magical place which commanded respect from all who ventured onto it.

In contrast, the summit of Helvelyn is a broad convex dome, scattered with small rocks but otherwise smooth. Several cairns, pillars and monuments have been erected over the years, the most interesting being a small plate commemorating the landing of an aeroplane in 1926.

Another plate records a second fatal accident on Striding Edge, and the Ordnance Survey pillar, placed on the highest point, confirms to all travellers that they have made the true summit.

Nearby, a very convenient shelter provides relief from the winds. A stone wall, pointing four ways in the shape of a cross, guarantees that whichever way the wind is blowing, one can always find peace on the other side to unpack the sandwiches.

Jeff stretched out alongside the wall.

"That was some walk!"

It had indeed been a walk to remember. They would surely return one day and climb Helvelyn again.

"Over Striding Edge of course!"

HELVELYN FACTFILE

Helvelyn - 3118 ft   Moderate/Difficult
Third Highest summit in England
Nearest towns - Patterdale, Grasmere
Natural features - Two fine ridge routes, Striding Edge and Swirral Edge
Red Tarn

Blencathra

"This is a good one - Straight up Hall's Fell onto Blencathra."

Doug traced the route with his finger and looked up from the map.

"It's a bit sharp! Shall we have a go?"

"What's the alternative?" enquired Jeff.

"The easy way," Doug replied, "is from the other end, but you'll miss the best bit."

Irvin reached for the map, and Roy leaned over his shoulder.

"Looks OK to me."

"And me."

"Right, straight up Hall's Fell, then!"

Hall's Fell is, to many a seasoned mountaineer, the only classic way of climbing Blencathra. This is a unique mountain, always picturesque, offering a blend of two distinctly different types of walking.

Approaching from either flank, the walker finds a smooth, green ascent, a delightfully easy walk with outstanding views towards nearby Keswick, or to Penrith, some ten miles to the east. Those seeking excitement, however, will probably choose one of the southern approaches, a selection of exhilarating ridge climbs rising abruptly from the plain, thrusting upwards between deep eroded valleys, to reach the summit in an airy span of naked rock.

Hall's Fell is the pick of these ridges.

Doug and his party left the car in Threlkeld, just off the main Keswick road, and launched themselves into the first steep section of the climb.

"I suddenly feel very unfit," Jeff exclaimed.

"That's what sitting at a desk does for you," Doug pointed out. "Try fifty paces and take a breather." Roy didn't speak. He was too busy panting and trying to look composed.

Half an hour passed, and Jeff collapsed into the heather.

"Fifty paces you said. That last section was like the side of a house."

"Look on the bright side," Doug replied, looking as fresh as he did when he set off. "You've done the hard bit."

An outcrop of rocks brought a welcome diversion and slowed down the pace. It was not difficult climbing, but Doug and Irvin insisted on exchanging cameras half way up.

"Take one of me!"

"And me!"

It was positively hazardous for delicate photographic equipment to be swung about with gay abandon whilst clinging onto a rock face with one hand.

"Had you thought about keeping your own camera?" Roy suggested. "You can always exchange photos later."

"Mine's better than his," Doug retorted, nearly dropping the lot as he spoke.

Jeff poked his head over the rocks and gave a hoot, which announced the first sighting of the ridge ahead. It was suddenly worth all the effort of getting there, a snaking chain of sharp edges winding up to the summit.

Occasionally a rough, grassy track would pass a difficult section, slightly lower than the crest, sometimes to the left, then to the right, but everyone tried to keep as much as possible to the highest flakes of rock, enjoying the sheer delight of exposed scrambling.

On both sides the empty space of the deep barren valleys appeared spectacular. The jumbled rocks strewn along the dry stream courses seemed a million miles away, and occasionally, floating on the wind, there would be the distant clink of rock as a mountain sheep clattered clumsily over the terrain.

The scene was ablaze with Autumn colours, yellows and browns in vivid streaks and subtle pastel shades,

Blencathra

following the line of the screes down to the village of Threlkeld.

In complete contrast, the black pyramid of Hall's Fell Top dominated the skyline ahead, reminding the party that there was some hard work still to do. The wind was beginning to gust fiercely, and could be heard whistling past the higher crags not far ahead.

The last section of the ridge was the fulfilment of all they had set out to find, a selection of delicate manoeuvres around rocky turrets, rough scrambles over knife-edge flakes and careful climbs on naked towers of crumbling stone.

Doug had been reading his guide book. "They call this Narrow Edge," he announced. "It says the locals don't come up here very often."

Come to think of it, they hadn't seen anyone at all since setting off that morning, not even on the summit ridges ahead. It was unusual not to see tourists around.

"Visitors usually want to climb Scafell or Helvelyn," Irvin explained. "Blencathra is more on the edge of the Lake District and doesn't get the traffic."

"Good thing too," Roy suggested.

Certainly Blencathra lacked the broad eroded tracks that deface most of the other mountains. Looking around from the lofty ridge of the fell, they could easily pick out Helvelyn, Causey Pike, Catbells and Skiddaw, and even spotted tourists, like little ants, crawling up the brown tracks that were fast becoming motorways, growing wider and wider with every season.

Back on Hall's Fell, the last airy scramble led the party onto the summit ridge, where the wind gusted strongly, and low clouds scudded past like express trains, occasionally enveloping them in a grey mist. A cairn of stones, roughly piled into a mound, told them that they had arrived at the highest point. This was the true summit of Blencathra, and everyone took out their flasks to celebrate with a drink of coffee. The wind was cold, and they hooded up their anoraks, clutching tightly to their flask tops to prevent them being whisked away into the valley.

"Can't hang around here very long," Irvin remarked.

"Pardon?" Roy leaned over to catch what he said, but conversation was not possible. Roy could see Irvin's lips moving, but the words were taken away in the wind.

Doug led off, and they strode along the summit ridge, leaning into the gale as they fought to keep on their feet. The views to the valley were awe-inspiring, made more dramatic by the precipice at their feet, overlooking the yawning void of Doddick Gill.

Their one concern was to ensure that the wind did not take them over the edge, and it seemed sensible to forsake the view for a safer path a few yards down from the crest. The relief was immediate, and the gale subsided to about force eight.

Irvin pointed to the next high point along the summit, another cairn of stones marking the end of the plateau.

"That's where we go down onto Sharp Edge," he explained. "It's a bit steeper than Hall's Fell. You'll love it!"

The grassy depression between the two summits is known as the "saddle", which is seen to best effect from the east on the Penrith Road. Hence the mountain's alternative name "Saddleback," a name which the early explorers found more descriptive.

Walking along the saddle provided a little light relief from the intense scrambling of the first ascent, and it didn't take long to reach the cairn overlooking Sharp Edge.

"Hell, that's impossible!" Roy's first reaction was one of panic.

It was unreal - a wave of sharp rock, visibly tilted, with an alarming drop on its north side.

The southern aspect was only slightly better, plunging down a rock-strewn slope into Scales Tarn, a dark pool, nearly circular, nestling in the valley.

"Is it safe?" Jeff asked, looking at Doug for some reassurance.

"Should be OK," replied Doug, "if we stick together," and he began leading the party down towards the knife-edge.

The craggy track leading down from the summit ridge was itself a difficult proposition, having crumbled over the years to become a scree-filled gully, with sharp rocks waiting at every turn to tear at any loose clothing and inflict grazes on the unwary. It was a descent requiring great care.

Blencathra

Reaching the start of Sharp Edge was a relief. No bruises, no grazes, no loss of limbs! However, the next move turned out to be a tricky one.

A sloping rock had to be negotiated. Doug led the way, shuffling across on the seat of his pants.

"A bit polished," he remarked. "Careful you don't slip."

Progress became slow, and everyone crossed onto the knife-edge with some trepidation. Once over the initial move, they were able to use a small ledge just below the crest, holding onto the rim of the rock with both hands as they went.

The most awkward move was across a huge block of rock, more tilted than the rest. There was no obvious route over the top, and the sparse track below it had disappeared, so Doug had to hang onto the top edge and place the soles of his boots against the side of the rock, shuffling crab-like across its face.

"It's worse than Striding Edge," Jeff shouted, as he gripped the top and tried to find somewhere to put his feet.

"Hold it!" shouted Irvin, pointing the camera, but Jeff wasn't feeling inclined to hang around too long for a photograph. He was most relieved to gain the safer ground at the far end of the obstruction.

This was a good place to pause and take stock of the situation. They tried to convince themselves that the worst part was behind them. The rocks over which they had just climbed curled upwards in a wave towards the bulk of the mountain, eventually becoming lost in a jumble of loose rock and scree.

The whole length of the Edge was very similar, requiring a firm hold with the hands on the top, and careful placing of the boots. They tried to ignore the alarming drop below.

Hanging on desperately, it was possible to look down between the knees and see nothing but jagged rocks and scree.

The wind still howled fiercely, and the next blast could be heard approaching somewhere down-valley, roaring like an express train, growing louder with every second, until suddenly it struck. This caused everyone to drop onto the rocks, grabbing anything within reach, until the ferocity subsided enough to continue safely.

Eventually they found themselves between two large blocks of rock, and stopped to recover their composure. Knees, which had turned to jelly, slowly gathered strength, and they continued over a rough but easy track until they were able to look back and say, "Well done, that was a stinker!"

The rest of the day's walk was easy, losing height very quickly on steep grassy hillsides. For the last couple of miles they followed an enchanting stream back towards the peaceful village of Threlkeld.

It was some years later when Roy returned to explore the western flank of Blencathra. Having already seen the rugged fells on the southern and eastern sides, he was determined to complete his experience with a reconnaissance of the smoother approach, Blease Fell.

"I'll take the long ridge to the summit," he thought. "Great views along the way."

It was going to be a memorable and very unusual day, although he didn't know it when he began his journey at 9 o'clock on a wet Tuesday morning in May.

Overnight rain had lashed the Lake District with the ferocity of a tropical storm, and continued through breakfast-time, until the streets ran like rivers.

It was nearly ten o'clock when he parked his car near Threlkeld, thankful that the rain had eased somewhat. Although the sky looked brighter to the west, it felt bitterly cold in the wind.

Cloud base was down to about 1500 feet, completely hiding the upper slopes of the mountain. Nevertheless, he set off with high hopes of the weather clearing completely, and was pleased to find that his windproof cagoule was keeping him quite warm, especially after half an hour's exertion.

Just as he thought, on reaching 1500 feet, the cloud base engulfed him, obscuring everything. The way ahead was confused by a dull grey mist, in which he could just pick out the track winding uphill through the grass and heather.

"Don't do anything stupid," he told himself. "You're on your own today!"

Blencathra

The wind still blew strongly from the north, making it feel extremely cold. The rain was still driving across, and there were crystals of ice in it, cutting into his cheeks.

"I must be mad," he cursed loudly, "Completely off my rocker!"

He felt better when he realised the terrain was not difficult, and the track continued on a winding course, mainly over grass, with the occasional clump of heather, and a scattering of loose rocks where erosion had removed the top layer of soil.

There was slushy ice on the grass as he climbed higher, evidence that it had been snowing during the night.

"Yes, I thought it felt cold enough for it," Roy thought, searching for his gloves.

Then he noticed that there were flakes of snow still falling around him, and not far ahead in the mist, it looked very much whiter on the ground.

He pulled the hood further over his face until only his nose was showing.

Soon he estimated that he must have climbed to about 2000 feet. Three inches of new snow covered the path, hiding the clumps of heather and protruding rocks. It was a time to take care where he put his feet.

Marching on through the cloud, he noticed that the track was beginning to level out a little, and not far to the right he could see the ground dropping away over a cliff edge.

"Knowe Crags," he said aloud. He'd seen it on the map that morning. Leaving the safe path, he wandered over to have a look.

Below the crags was a huge basin, gouged out of the mountain by ice-age glaciers.

A miniature hurricane was howling down there. He could hear it. Strong enough here on the ridge, but it sounded worse down there. Suddenly the wind turned up the face of the rock, gusting past Roy's ears like the scream of a passing jet plane, bringing with it long streamers of cloud, with rain, sleet and snow for good measure.

He staggered back from the impact, feeling to see if his nose was still there, and stood for a moment wiping tears from his face, tears which had blown back along his frozen cheeks into his ears.

Keeping a few yards from the edge, he continued along the line of crags, knowing that this was the start of the summit ridge. The cairn on the true summit was about a mile ahead. It was obviously going to take some time in the bleak conditions. Worse still, he could see only ten yards in front of him, and there didn't seem to be any prospect of seeing any worth-while views.

Snow cover was about six inches, maybe more, and large flakes spun around in the wind as he trudged on. There were no footprints, no hint that anyone else had gone that way. He was alone on a snowy mountain, an eerie feeling of isolation, but one which gave him tremendous satisfaction. He experienced a rare affinity with the mountain, a sense that Blencathra was his today, and his alone!

"One, two three..." he counted, trying to measure distance in paces as he trudged onwards. "Three miles per hour... No, two miles per hour today. Should be there about twelve o'clock."

An hour later he saw a dark shape ahead, which he guessed was the summit cairn at just over 2800 feet.

"It feels more like 28 *thousand* feet today," he thought, brushing snow and slush from his waterproofs. "This isn't really happening!"

The situation was bleak. Snow swept across in sheets, the wind howled continuously at gale force. Brief thoughts crossed his mind, thoughts about "wind chill," and the vision of frost-bite, even though it was an afternoon in May, somewhere in sunny England!

He could not remember ever experiencing conditions like these in his years as a mountaineer, and he smiled as this thought gave him more satisfaction. He was extremely *lucky* to be here today. A feeling of triumph!

Looking over the abrupt edge, he recognised the well-known route of Hall's Fell, which fell away from the ridge at that point. This confirmed his navigation. How different it looked, compared with the last time he had climbed it on a sunny Autumn day.

"Lunchtime!" he announced, addressing a sorry-looking sheep with lumps of frozen slush hanging from its wool. "That makes two of us!" he added, but the sheep wandered slowly away, apparently having seen enough.

Blencathra

Roy had hoped to find some shelter near the summit, but there wasn't a wall, a crag, or a hollow anywhere. There was no respite from the weather, and it was beginning to feel colder than ever now he had stopped moving.

The only solution was his survival bag, which he always kept in his rucksack. It was only a six-foot plastic bag, with air holes punched in it, but it proved to be almost a life-saver as he sat under it, eating his sandwiches. For a few moments he enjoyed the relative calm inside.

"It's two coats warmer in here," he thought, almost breaking his teeth on an icy sandwich.

Packing up for the return journey, he noticed that the snow had stopped, but the cold hadn't relented one little bit. Nevertheless, he resolved to have a photograph to remember the occasion, and spent five minutes trying to balance the camera on a prominent rock to take a delayed action shot. By the time he had finished, his fingers had gone completely white and lost all feeling.

"Frost-bite," he thought, looking at his lifeless hands, and walked for the next twenty minutes with them tucked under his armpits to thaw them out. The numbness gradually disappeared, to be replaced by the excruciating pain of restarted circulation.

"Sunshine!" Roy strode out more quickly as the mist cleared. He carried his camera in his hand, ready for action.

At last, the clouds were breaking. Suddenly he could see the valley again, beautiful and green. A hazy warmth was even beginning to percolate through the clouds on Blencathra, lighting up the winter scene on the ridge.

There was just one line of footprints - his own. Not another soul had set foot on the mountain that day. Even these tracks were beginning to disappear as the temperature rose, and soon Roy was marching down Blease Fell through green grass in the warm rays of the afternoon sun.

On his way back to Keswick, he called at Castle Rigg to see the picturesque setting of the Stone Circle. Just across the valley, the whole Blencathra range was displayed in the sunshine, and not a trace of snow to be seen anywhere!

It was the perfect picture of a friendly mountain, and as Roy paused to take a last photograph, one compelling thought crossed his mind. Nobody else could ever guess what Blencathra had been like on that morning in May.

BLENCATHRA FACTFILE

Blencathra - 2847 ft.   Moderate/Difficult
Also known as Saddleback
Nearest Towns - Keswick, Threlkeld
Features - Two fine ridge routes,
            Hall's Fell and Sharp Edge

Holme Moss

Holme Moss -
Winter walk, from the snow-bound village of Holme

featured in a following chapter, page 57

Reproductions from water colour originals
by Roy Bedford ©

Borrowdale

Hindscarth - Robinson
The Borrowdale approach reveals the scars of many abandoned slate quarries, copper mines and ruined buildings

featured in a following chapter, page 62

Reproductions from water colour originals
by Roy Bedford ©

Hindscarth

Hindscarth,
circular walk from Newlands to Robinson

featured in a following chapter, page 62

Reproductions from water colour originals
by Roy Bedford ©

Scafell Pike

Scafell Pike and Scafell

Scafell Pike, on the left, is fractionally higher, linked to Scafell by the tortuous Lords Rake

featured in a following chapter, page 69

Reproductions from water colour originals
by Roy Bedford ©

Grange

Grange Bridge, Borrowdale
Once seen, always remembered

Many a good walk finishes at Grange

Reproductions from water colour originals
by Roy Bedford ©

Pavey Ark

Pavey Ark, Langdale.
The infamous Jack`s Rake is the fault line
running from bottom right to top left

featured in a following chapter, Page 69

Reproductions from water colour originals
by Roy Bedford ©

Loughrigg

Loughrigg and its tarn

featured in a following chapter, page 53

Reproductions from water colour originals
by Roy Bedford ©

Eagle Crag

*Eagle Crag
dominating the Stonethwaite Valley, Borrowdale*

featured in a following chapter, page 73

Reproductions from water colour originals
by Roy Bedford ©

Helm Crag

Helm Crag is a truly modest mountain, only 1300 feet in height, surrounded by magnificent peaks towering to twice the elevation. So often the walker will travel between Keswick and Ambleside, looking for a great mountain challenge, not realising that the charm of Helm Crag is there to be explored, only a mile from the village of Grasmere.

Visitors to the village must choose between the attractions of the hills, the charm of the stone cottages, or the tranquility of Grasmere Lake, nestling between smooth fells of heather and bracken. Each Springtime, the yellow glow of kingcups sets the banks alight. Then in the Autumn the rust and gold of the trees transform the scene to one of warmth and richness.

It was late September when Roy and Irvin drove into the village, little realising that it was going to be a day of surprises. They were about to learn what variety and natural beauty a modest mountain can offer.

Leaving the main car park, they spent a pleasant hour looking round Grasmere, admiring the quaint stone buildings, colourful gardens, and the babbling stream which meanders through the village beneath old arched bridges.

Then Irvin looked at his watch and decided it was time they were moving. The way to Helm Crag was flanked by stone walls and tidy hedgerows. Roy remarked upon the well-kept gardens of the old cottages, and wondered about the idyllic existence of living in such a quiet backwater.

"You'd never survive," Irvin remarked. "It's a different life."

"Just give me one chance!" Roy grinned.

Soon they found the track they were looking for, leading off the lane. Towering majestically above the trees, Helm Crag now appeared much closer. On its flanks the Autumn colours of the bracken glowed in the midday sun.

The first part of the ascent was steep, and Irvin declared that since he didn't have a bus to catch, he would take the climb in short sections, pausing to admire the view at every opportunity. This suited Roy admirably, having brought his camera to make the most of the sunny conditions.

"Very well used, this path," observed Roy, struggling to maintain a foothold in the gravel that had once been a hard track.

"You and your big boots," Irvin retorted. "You're removing more topsoil than a flock of mountain sheep!"

Roy pondered briefly over the possibility of driving a flock of sheep up this steep track, but couldn't see what that would achieve. Too much like hard work, anyway.

They reached the summit ridge without any major difficulties, and stood for a short while admiring the aerial view of Grasmere and the lake beyond. The stone walls and green fields of the valley made a pleasant picture, spread like a map below them.

At each end of the ridge there were prominent rock formations. The first of these was a sloping wedge of rock overhanging the steep slope, and in its shadow was the shattered debris which must at one time have been part of the original wedge.

Irvin pointed to the leaning formation. "You see the front edge of that one," he said, making a curving motion with his hand. "That's the lion, and the small rock over there is the lamb."

Roy looked at them thoughtfully. "That's right! It's in Wainwright's book. It says you can see it from the village."

Irvin led the way across the ridge to the far end, where a much larger rock formation stood guard over the steep northern flank of the hill. This was an awesome feature, a spectacular wedge of weathered rock protruding high above the ridge at an acute angle, its highest point actually overhanging the valley.

Helm Crag

It was not difficult to imagine this, too, as a lion, towering majestically into the clouds. The hillside immediately below the crag was split by a deep cleft, half filled with loose stones, and beyond the cleft a smaller rock could possibly have been another "lamb."

The dark shadows in the depths of the cleft gave the crag a sinister appearance, and Roy was filled with great feelings of trepidation as he explored all around. Just as he was working his way round below the crag at the steepest point, he was surprised to find a lone mountain ash, clinging precariously to a crack in the rock.

Swaying in the teeth of the gale, its leaves had been completely stripped off, leaving a good crop of orange berries. It was the only tree in sight for miles, and he wondered how it had possibly managed to take root in such a lofty position. Birds, perhaps?

Meanwhile, Irvin tried to find a way up the face of the main rock.

It was not a technically difficult climb, but the fierce wind threatened to tear him off, and he clung on desperately. His clothing flapped noisily, and his yellow bob-cap nearly blew off into Grasmere as he neared the top. There was no chance of standing on the highest pinnacle today. Nevertheless, he managed to coax Roy into following him, and together they hung on, speechless, head and shoulders above the rock, trying to hold a camera steady.

Clambering down from the high point, they sought shelter below the crag, and stayed five minutes or so to enjoy the flasks of coffee which they always carried with them.

Hot drinks! These were always well appreciated, but they hadn't yet managed to find a flask which was large enough to contain a decent supply of drinks, yet light enough to carry in the rucksack.

Irvin looked through the guide book.

"Hey, just listen to this," he announced. "Four different names for the same rock! The Lion and the Lamb, the Lion Couchant, the Howitzer, and the Old Woman playing the Organ."

"Old Woman?" exclaimed Roy. "I don't see any woman."

"No, you have to be across the other side of the valley, on the approaches to Fairfield," Irvin explained. "Then the main rock becomes the Organ, and one of these pointed rocks becomes the Old Woman."

Roy leaned across to look at the illustration. It did look like the silhouette of a figure, but he wasn't convinced. He resolved to have a look from the other viewpoint one day.

Shouldering their rucksacks again, they wandered off the main ridge, and had a look at the valleys and cracks in the steep side of the fell, where grassy depressions gave the appearance of stone-age defences. The book made no mention of any ancient activity, and Roy concluded that the formations must be natural.

"Erosion," said Irvin.

"Ice Age," added Roy.

They concluded that over a period of time, the ravages of snow and frost had split the rock into slices, which had slipped, leaving deep abysses along the line of the fractures. Loose rock and soil had partly filled them, forming grassy terraces just below the rim of the ridge.

Today, these are stable and safe, pleasantly sheltered from the wind, and command a fantastic view of the valley, overlooking the main Keswick road.

The Helvelyn/Fairfield range dominates the north-eastern skyline, standing proudly, twice the height of Helm Crag - a completely different proposition. On a good day, groups of people can be seen, like ants, crawling up the main tourist paths. Then, on a stormy Winter's day you don't see anyone at all.

That is where Helm Crag wins. It is a walk for all seasons. The crag is seldom unfriendly, and whichever time of the year one chooses to climb, the reward is unparalleled, a walk full of interest and variation.

"How about doing this in January?" Roy suggested.

"Sure thing! We'll bring the kids..."

"And Granny?"

HELM CRAG FACTFILE

Helm Crag - 1299 ft.   Easy walking
Nearest town - Grasmere
Features - Two summit formations, both commonly known as The Lion and the Lamb

The Cobbler

Those who head north by Loch Lomond and Loch Long, looking for the climbing centres of Fort William and the Isle of Skye, will certainly pass close by this mountain. The main road climbs up from Loch Long, over the "Rest and be Thankful" Pass, with unforgettable views of Scottish hills, forests and lakes. There, on the right at the top of the pass is The Cobbler, listed on most maps and motoring guides as "Ben Arthur, 2891 ft".

On a clear day, the sight of those barren crags rising from the summit will strike fear into the casual walker, inspire curiosity in the hoards of tourists and sightseers, and throw out a challenge to the seasoned climber, as if to say, "Afore ye pass, come and see me, aye, and ye'll nae regret it!"

Ben Arthur gets its popular name "The Cobbler" from the shape of the crags which dominate the summit, and at a certain angle the visitor can detect the head of a busy shoemaker, working on his anvil. It is difficult to imagine this from any point on the road, but those who venture onto the mountain will be impressed by the cobbler's presence, and terrified by the prospect of surmounting the final vertical crags.

Roy, Doug and Irvin arrived on a sunny September evening at a camp site near the small town of Arrochar, pitching their tents by the waterside at Loch Long. They were pleased with the position, and the adequate facilities offered at the site, but had completely forgotten the reputation of the Scottish midge, a voracious little creature with an insatiable appetite for blood. Here on the shores of the Loch, they descended like a plague, covering everything in a black layer, moving over every unprotected surface.

"Hell, that's a full bottle of repellant - gone in two minutes," Irvin exclaimed.

The Cobbler was the week's prime objective. It was just visible on the skyline above the woods, and on the morning of the walk, the crags appeared fleetingly between the clouds. Sunshine warmed the scene as they prepared their rucksacks and put on their boots.

"What's the forecast?" Doug asked, noticing that Irvin had tuned in to his car radio.

"Showers this afternoon, could be on the heavy side. Get your brollies out!"

They opted for heavy waterproof anoraks, which soon felt uncomfortable as the party set out on foot from the camp site, and within half an hour they had stripped them off, tying them onto the top of their rucksacks.

The pine woods of the lower slopes were a delight for leisurely walking. The footing was good and dry, cushioned by layers of pine needles, making the tread soft and easy.

Higher on the mountain-side, young pines had been planted to in-fill where timber had been extracted, and to extend the forestry plantations upwards. Here the branches of the growing trees formed inpenetrable barriers in places, and the party had to force their way through the undergrowth. Sharp needles snatched at the corners of loose clothing, caught on the straps of rucksacks, and threatened to scratch out the eyes of the unwary.

Eventually the woods opened out into areas of heather and tufted grass, and Doug chose a route going obliquely uphill, heading for the end of the ridge which they could see clearly on the skyline.

Shower clouds were beginning to form on the hilltops, and the morning sunshine was rapidly disappearing.

Loch Long, a narrow inlet of the sea, stretched away to the south-west, and a silvery glow on the distant horizon hinted at sunlight on the Irish Sea.

To the west, heavy cloud had formed a thick continuous sheet, a dramatic black lid clamped down onto the mountain tops, squeezing down upon the sandwich of gleaming light striking through from the coast.

"The Cobbler's disappeared," Doug remarked.

"Yeah," Roy added, "Weather's closing in."

The Cobbler

Mountain sheep peered at the group from every angle. Most of them were very untidy in their thick, tangled Autumn coats, and seemed ready for the onset of Winter, when a good protective layer would be essential to keep out the Scottish snow and wind. It was interesting to watch them shuffle along, carrying a great weight of matted wool, heavy with rainwater and mud.

They were often seen on the skyline, head and shoulders above, like "injuns" in the old Westerns, a dozen at a glance. At every corner, with every new scene, there would be scores more of them, and Roy felt as though he was being watched.

"Look out!" he warned. "We're going to be ambushed."

They continued uphill, keeping the same line towards the end of the ridge, encountering large areas of bog, and small streams running across their path every hundred yards or so. The ground was extremely soft after the heavy rain of the last few weeks, and some of the bog was deep, clutching hard at their boots as they tried to progress through it.

The streams were partly hidden by overgrowing grass, as Doug discovered when he broke through into a foot of icy water, collapsing onto the wet grass in an undignified prostrate position.

This rough treatment did nothing for the appearance of boots and trousers, and they tried hard to convince each other that this was just the job for a September afternoon. Much better than sitting at a desk drinking cups of tea.

"I can understand why the mountain sheep look like dirty mops," Irvin remarked.

Reaching the shoulder of the ridge, they found that as the ground levelled off the bogs became even more extensive. Outcrops of rock stretched across their path, slowing progress, and calling for great care as they picked their way over the slippery lichen and moss.

Doug stopped again to survey the sky, which had become very dark. Drops of rain pattered on their anoraks, and murky cloud began to descend onto the ridge.

"Looks like we're gonna get it," he observed.

"Just a shower," Roy suggested, always the optimist.

It didn't look very good. The first raindrops passed, but there was an inky blackness to the sky which suggested quite a bit of rain to come. The one consoling factor was that the surrounding mountain tops were nearly all visible, so the walk wasn't going to be a complete washout.

To the east, they could pick out Ben Lomond, towering above the loch which bears the same name. The misty summit looked majestic above the smooth dark blue water, where a hint of sunshine still lingered.

They surmounted yet another outcrop of rocks, clambering onto a wet, grassy surface above it, and caught sight of the summit crag, the head of the Cobbler. It seemed very near, and what a forbidding sight it looked!

Steep faces soared upwards, rugged and sheer, and the head appeared to overhang. Nothing but empty space below - it looked impossible.

Clouds descended once more, obliterating the crags, and rain began to drive across on the increasing wind. Irvin was quick to take action, leading the retreat behind a large group of rocks, where he found a particularly large one leaning conveniently away from the prevailing wind. The hollow behind it was dry, and Roy imagined that this rock could well have been the salvation of many a walking party on that wet mountain.

Huddled as far under the rock as they could get, they watched as the low cloud dropped over the Cobbler's shoulder into the valley, obscuring the peaks on the opposite side. Rain fell in long vertical sheets, and ice bounced around their feet.

"I've heard the old saying - raining like stair rods," Doug remarked, "but this is the first time I've been in it."

They could clearly see the rain leaving the cloud base in solid lines, just like somebody turning a tap fully on. The bogs and muddy holes around them were rapidly filling with water, and the grass was turning patchy white with melting ice from the hailstones.

The cloud passed as abruptly as it had come, and Irvin led the way across the ridge towards the crags, his boots squelching in the wet grass as he went.

"It's not the grass you can hear, it's my socks," he explained. "They need wringing out."

The crags came into view again, and it became apparent that there were two features, one at each end of the summit. The Cobbler's head was by far the more dramatic of the two, and Roy suggested that they just

The Cobbler

concentrate on that one. In truth, he was a little worried about the wind, which was screaming at gale force through the gap between the two crags. He felt that if they managed to climb just one of them, they would have done enough for one day.

Whispy clouds raced past the top of the crags, making them look even higher and steeper.

The height of the Cobbler is enough to dismay even the most seasoned climber, but it is possible to cheat! A rocky track winds its way up the back of it, offering an easy ascent without loss of life or limb.

Doug was the first to try it. He was delighted to find that once on the twisting track, the wind was less troublesome, and he was able to lead the party up to a high vantage point where they could see the main features of the crag.

The Anvil of the Cobbler protruded above the valley, a spur of rock narrowing almost to a point, with a slab of stone balanced precariously at the very tip. It would have been possible to walk out to the stone, but they didn't want to indulge in any acrobatics, as the wind was so unpredictable, and the rock was rather greasy with lichen. Clearly not the place to hang around too long, so they retreated, rejoining the twisting track.

After a few yards, they arrived at a deep crack cutting across their path. The mountain was split, revealing a clean gap, separating the Anvil from the head of the Cobbler.

Doug stood astride the narrow end, looking down between his legs. The empty space was awesome, and the very act of looking downwards made his head dizzy. He retreated again, preferring the safety of the track.

After a couple of hurried photographs, they continued upwards until they reached the point where it levelled out at the summit.

This was the top of the Cobbler's head, an area of smooth rock, about the size of a small kitchen. It was slightly tilted, with a rough cairn of stones marking the high point at the far end.

The wind howled relentlessly as Doug crossed towards the cairn, and he crouched low as he scuttled over the wet surface. Too hasty! About half way across, his feet slipped on a patch of green moss, and he landed on his posterior, spinning and sliding over the greasy rock.

He let out a strangled cry as he slipped towards the edge, flailing his arms across the wet rock in an effort to find something to hold on to.

In the nick of time his hand located a small crack, and he hung there for a moment before crawling over to the cairn.

Doug's face was grey with shock, and it was a few seconds before he could draw breath to speak.

"Hell, I just saw my past life flashing before me," he croaked.

With extreme care the others followed, taking a route near the top of the slope, where the rock seemed drier. Soon they were all sitting around the cairn, keeping a tight hold to prevent the wind from blowing them away.

They remained there for a couple of minutes, hardly saying anything as they regained their breath. What a precarious position! It was like sitting on the top of the cathedral spire.

Being the last one on, Roy had to be first off, and led the way back down the track, back to the safety of the bogs. How friendly they looked! Even the black peaty holes were a blessing after the exposure of the Cobbler's head.

They looked at the other crag, at the far end of the summit ridge, undecided whether to climb that one too, but after a brief discussion the onset of rain made it a simple choice. In those conditions it was not going to be worth the effort, and they set off down the mountain side with hoods up and leggings on.

The clouds descended, and heavy rain continued for the rest of the walk. The Cobbler disappeared into the blackness of the storm to await another day, and perhaps another group of unsuspecting tourists!

COBBLER FACTFILE

The Cobbler - 2891 ft.   Moderate/Difficult
Also known as Ben Arthur
Nearest Towns - Arrochar, Inveraray
Nearest Pass - Rest and be Thankful
Features - Dramatic summit crags, The Cobbler

Mardale

The village of Mardale Green suddenly became famous and enjoyed a few weeks of the limelight during the Summer of 1984.

It had been one of those rare years when the north-west had enjoyed the best of the weather. According to the Met men, an anticyclone had become stationary over Western Scotland, bringing continuous sunshine and long, hot, sunny days. The grass turned yellow, streams and tarns dried up completely, and the local gardeners could only watch as their neatly kept lawns and borders turned to dust.

The public water supply was reaching crisis point, which was almost unknown in the history of the Lake District. But more significantly, the Manchester area relied on some of the lakes for their main source of fresh water, and the sudden threat to these supplies resulted in a state of panic in the city.

Camera crews from the local television networks converged on the reservoirs, and quickly discovered that Haweswater was the one most dramatically affected by the drought.

Haweswater Reservoir, as it is now known, was created in the late 1930's, when a smaller lake was enlarged, flooding the entire valley. For the next forty years the new lake was a sparkling sea of water, always full to overflowing, a permanent and plentiful supply for the industries, commerce and communities of Lancashire.

1984, however, saw a dramatic change in the valley. The streams feeding the reservoir were reduced to a trickle, and the water level began to recede rapidly. It was just what the camera crews were looking for. The nation's viewers were treated to the unusual sight of a submerged village reappearing into sunlight for the first time in two generations.

It was Mardale Green!

The arch of the old packhorse bridge was seen protruding from the lake, and soon there were stone walls and country lanes, all emerging from the bed of the reservoir.

It was all too much. The tourists began to arrive in their thousands, all desperate to savour that moment of walking the streets of a village that they never knew, and would probably never see again.

The narrow single-carriage roads of Cumbria became jammed every day, to such an extent that many travellers never managed to get there, and those who had started early and reached the head of the valley found that they couldn't leave for several hours until the traffic had cleared. The police appealed to the nation to stay away and give the local community a chance to get on with their lives.

Roy waited until September, when the flush of tourists had diminished, and paid his respects to the site on a cold, grey Wednesday morning.

According to the newspapers, the water level was still receding despite the 30 million gallons pumped from Ullswater every day, and an additional 30 million gallons from Windermere. It had rained during the week, but not enough to swell the natural streams. The fells were so dry, it would take another month of rain before the water started flowing again.

As he drove alongside the lake, Roy noticed a few more cars heading the same way, to the head of the valley. It was obvious where they were going, and sure enough they all turned into the small car park. There were no crowds, no traffic jams, and no police, just a small group of tourists who had come to take photographs. Peace had returned to the valley.

Just down the road, another small group of cars were parked near the reservoir wall. Roy peered over the parapet, and there it was - the village!

Mardale

The scene was strangely painted in browns and greys, the effect of so many years under the water. There were roads, stone walls, and the heaps of jumbled stone which had once been cottages.

The pack-horse bridge still stood over the stream, where once again water flowed along the original course. The old arch was perfectly intact, although most of the parapet had vanished.

It was a strange, quiet scene, a dismal apparition of a dead village, where ghosts of the former inhabitants roamed slowly between ruined dwellings. The "ghosts" soon revealed themselves as tourists in brown duffel coats, carrying cameras.

"That's where I want to be," thought Roy. He had never known Mardale Green, yet the pathetic sight of the ruins attracted him. It was like a museum, a shrine to the memory of a departed community.

He clambered down below the brown line which indicated the high water level, and soon passed several groups of people coming up from the village. Some of them carried stones from the dry walls, souvenirs collected from the caked mud of the valley.

More tourists were wandering about the mud-covered roads and taking photographs of the unusual scenes. Another group were heading towards a conical hill that had once been an island in the reservoir. Concentric water lines ran around the contours of the hill, and the small clump of trees on its crest, normally a sanctuary for birds, were enjoying human visitors for the first time in many years.

But where was the water? Had it all disappeared, every last drop? Roy looked down the valley beyond the conical hill, and saw the brown surface of the reservoir about half a mile away. It was quite impossible to imagine the quantities of water which had drained away - Millions of gallons - Billions? - Trillions???

As he trod over the roads, the surface of caked mud crackled under his feet, and dust blew around in the warm, dry air. The fields were also dry and bare, cracked into a honeycomb pattern by the heat of the sun.

Then he noticed a faint green colour in the shade of the old walls. Kneeling down to investigate, he couldn't believe it - grass was beginning to establish itself. It was only two months since the waters had receded, but here it was - new grass! Only a microscopic layer of green, but it was definitely growing again.

He turned the corner into the lane which led to the old packhorse bridge, and here the tarmac of the road was visible, where so many people had walked in the last few weeks. The bridge itself was almost clear of mud, and the stonework was as good and sound as it must have been in its heyday. It was sad, however, to see how much of the parapet had disappeared. These stones must have been prime targets for the souvenir hunters.

Below the archway, the original stream course was flowing with fresh water. "That will be the water from Ullswater," Roy thought, and remembered the line of pipes and pumping stations he had once seen on the hills towards Patterdale.

He looked around at the high sides of the reservoir, ringed with water lines marking the various levels from year to year. It was a creepy feeling, knowing that he was perhaps thirty feet below the highest line.

Walking over the bridge, he soon passed the heaps of stone where the houses and church once stood. It was hard to imagine how these confused jumbles of rock had been tidy cottages, with roses and foxgloves blooming in their small gardens. It was impossible to say which was the church, and the beautiful trees and hedgerows had long since gone. The scene was dull, brown and cheerless.

Roy followed the lane downhill. Most of the stone walls were intact, but the road surface was buried beneath a thick layer of dark mud, which became wetter and wetter as he walked away from the village. Soon he was sinking into a deep layer of wet silt, and it was not possible to go any further.

The road continued into the receding water, disappearing under the brown surface. The stone walls flanking the lane ran on for another hundred yards, until they, too, disappeared into the reservoir. The four miles of water beyond that point must have engulfed many more walls, cottages and farms, which are unlikely ever to be seen again.

He retraced his steps past the ruined cottages, over the bridge, and up towards the car park.

Mardale

The weather was changing, and low cloud had already descended over the hills. Soon the patter of large raindrops sent everyone scurrying for shelter, and Roy retreated to the warmth of the car.

He took out his sandwiches and slowly ate his lunch, reflecting on the sad scenes he had witnessed in the valley bottom.

The storm broke, and as the rain lashed against the windscreen, Roy could do nothing but wait. He watched with some trepidation as the car park became a sea of running water.

The last of the tourists were disappearing.

Roy paid another visit to the valley during the early Spring. As he looked over the stone wall of the car park he was amazed to see the difference. The reservoir was full!

Where he had previously looked down into the village, it was now water, just clear blue water, lapping the stones which mark the rim of the reservoir.

The conical hill had become an island once more, and the packhorse bridge was out of sight, thirty feet below the surface.

Who knows? It may be another forty years before the village of Mardale Green is seen again.

MARDALE FACTFILE

Mardale - Sunken village in Haweswater Lake.
Village demolished in 1936, flooded the following Winter to form a reservoir for Manchester.
Nearest towns - Shap, Bampton.
Features - (ruins of) - Dun Bull Inn, Holy Trinity Church, Old Measand School.
Chapel Hill, also known as Wood Howe, now an island.

Pictures, page 41:

Haweswater, the reservoir which used to be a small lake, now a source of fresh water for the industrial areas of Lancashire.

The remains of Mardale Green, once a quiet Lakeside village, submerged for 40 years under the rising water.

Mardale

Snowdon

*Snowdon
seen on the approach from Betws-y-Coed*

featured in a following chapter, page 65

Reproductions from water colour originals
by Roy Bedford ©

Ambleside

The Bridge House, Ambleside

Hindscarth

Hindscarth -
The ridge to Hindscarth and Robinson

featured in a following chapter, page 62

Reproductions from water colour originals
by Roy Bedford ©

Stonethwaite

Stonethwaite -
The idyllic valley leading to Eagle Crag

featured in a following chapter, page 73

Reproductions from water colour originals
by Roy Bedford ©

The Bishop of Barf

featured in a following chapter, page 77

Great Gable

Great Gable

featuring the famous Napes Needle, page 80

Reproductions from water colour originals
by Roy Bedford ©

Stockley Bridge

*Stockley Bridge,
on the ascent from Borrowdale
to Great Gable*

featured in a following chapter, page 80

Reproductions from water colour originals
by Roy Bedford ©

Buttermere

The Buttermere valley is refreshingly quiet and completely unspoilt. By road there are only two common approaches. The easy one is from the Cumbrian coast in the west. The more scenic route, however, is over the Honister Pass from Borrowdale.

The huge block of the north-western fells separates this valley from the hustle and bustle of Windermere and Keswick, and this isolation has maintained the privacy of Buttermere. The connoisseur will find beauty and excitement here, where the twin lakes of Buttermere and Crummock Water sparkle in the clearness of a sunny day.

Roy arrived in Buttermere village on a typical English summer's morning in the middle of a rather damp July, when the sun couldn't make up its mind whether to shine or not.

Dismissing the obvious challenges of Robinson and High Stile, he picked Whiteless Pike, a rather steep but shorter climb from the village, with the reward of some good ridge walking if the weather held. In the event of rain, it was near enough to return to the village before he got too wet. Little did he know that circumstances were about to let him in for another soaking.

Whiteless Pike was tough for someone who usually sits at a desk all day. Roy found that he was onto the steep gradient within minutes of leaving the car park, and would have preferred an easier half-hour to loosen up before throwing himself at the tortuous section. Nevertheless, there he was, already perspiring freely in the humidity, and making steady progress up the well-trodden track towards the first shoulder of the hill.

Every hundred feet or so, he found an excuse to stop and look at the flora and fauna. It was just the day to appreciate the colours of the bracken and heather, and gaze at the bright patches of foxgloves lighting the hollows with their distinctive columns of pinky-mauve flowers. The hues of the wild flowers and bracken fronds seemed to stand out more in the milky light of oncoming rainclouds.

The thought of rain spurred him on to greater efforts, and with a supreme burst he made the top of the shoulder, having paused only once to tighten a bootlace.

The path levelled out slightly, then shot skywards for the last seven hundred feet to the summit. Roy looked up, saw what he had to do, and plodded on, hooding up his anorak as he went. Rain was beginning to wet the ground again, and he drew some consolation from the fact that the cooling rainwater would probably save him from the discomfort of getting too hot!

After a while, he paused again to survey the sky. The rain didn't seem to be getting any heavier, but he could see ragged clouds scudding past Scafell Pike, a few miles to the South, a sure sign of more rain to come. In fact, it did seem to be brighter overhead, but he was not easily fooled by that. He'd seen it all before - very often a break in the clouds is followed by heavy rain. It's about as predictable as the Grand National!

A man in a bright orange anorak appeared on the path ahead.

"Good day!" he announced.

"Yeah, super," Roy responded. "Come far?"

"Sort of," he replied. "I set off from Braithwaite over Causey Pike, and I'm going down into Buttermere now. About six miles this morning."

He looked young and fit, and seemed ready enough for another six, and another six after that! Rainwater ran off his waterproofs like a river, making his coat gleam in the murky light.

"I don't like the look of it," he said, motioning towards the west, shaking off quantities of water every time he moved.

Roy was conscious of cold rivulets running down his neck, and said that he would be looking for shelter now, and taking a lunch break.

Bidding Goodbye, the man splashed off down the slope, no doubt heading for the pub in Buttermere to dry off.

Buttermere

There was no sign of a break, the rain was heavier than ever, and his anorak was getting waterlogged round the bottom edge.

"I've got just the thing," he thought. "My cape!"

Perhaps by the time he had finished lunch the worst of the weather would have passed by. Having found a flattish rock, he sat down, removed his rucksack and searched for the cape.

Where was it? No cape!

He searched again, still no cape. He knew he had it. It was there yesterday, on his last walk. The wind had been so strong he had used it for shelter, but he could not remember what he had done with it after lunch. Was it possible that he had left it behind in the heather? Or perhaps it had blown away when his back was turned and he hadn't noticed.

Whichever way he looked at it, there was no cape, and here he was, high on a mountain in the pouring rain, with no shelter.

He stood astride the open rucksack, a tomato in one hand and a slice of bread in the other. Water was running down the inside of his shirt, and the bread was already beginning to get a little soggy at the edges. Nevertheless, he enjoyed his meal, and looked around the skyline for any sign of a break. It all looked about the same, and the mountains had mostly disappeared into the mist. Only the nearest peaks were visible, and even they looked as though they were merging into the cloud.

He weighed it all up. He was a little wet, but not uncomfortable, and definitely not cold. The day was only half over, and he felt physically able to complete the course. He would go on.

At this point, two young climbers, a man and a woman, came over the top. They carried heavy bundles of rope, and the clink of metal pitons and clips gave a clue to their exploits that day. They wore light coloured jumpers and jeans, which looked wetter than anything he had ever seen in his life - and that included washing day back home!

Roy was about to say "Good day" but thought he would just give them a nod instead. They didn't even bother to meet his glance. So many don't these days, many haven't got the time of day, but he thought that this couple needed a bright remark to lighten the situation.

Never mind, he thought, and continued uphill into the clouds.

The last hundred feet to the summit were perhaps the steepest of the lot. Determined to make good time from here on, Roy almost sprinted the last twenty yards, feeling as though it would tear his lungs apart.

Puffing and panting, he arrived at the cairn of stones, where a lakeland sheep was lying, like an enormous wet sponge, watching him with a look of complete boredom, as if to say "Oh no, here comes another one," chewing leisurely and trying to decide whether to get up or not.

The poor animal was obviously too heavy with rainwater. In any case there was a little warm dry patch underneath that soggy mat of wool, and she clearly wasn't going to relinquish it for anyone, let alone a solitary walker who hadn't even got a sheepdog with him!

This picture of complete relaxation and contentment contrasted sharply with Roy's own appearance - red-faced, short of breath and bathed in perspiration. What a way to enjoy life!

He decided to ignore the sheep, and stood for a few moments with one foot on the cairn, surveying his next move. There was a gradual ascent to Crag Hill, which looked very easy, and this would mark the half-way point in his walk. From there, a descending track would take him over the ridge of Scar Crag, down into the valley, and back to the car.

Scar Crag was everything he hoped it would be, a narrow ridge falling away two thousand feet on each side. It was easy walking, though, as the ridge was for the most part wide enough to drive a coach across.

There were wonderful views towards Buttermere, a panorama of steep-sided valleys, each ridge and buttress standing proudly, like something out of the Grand Canyon, hundreds of feet above the heather-clad valley bottom.

Somewhere in the distant green-ness below him, he could hear the trickle of a mountain stream. There would be plenty of water running down from the hills on that very wet day.

To his left, on the north side of the ridge, he could see nothing of the steep drop. Billowing grey cloud had descended into the valley on that side, and driven by the fierce wind, swirled up the rock face like an express train.

"It's that trick of the wind again," he thought,

Buttermere

remembering an almost identical phenomenon on Striding Edge a couple of years ago. Given the right conditions, it must be fairly common to see cloud on one side, and clear on the other.

The views towards Buttermere, however, remained clear despite the rain, and always dramatic. He paused many times to admire each new aspect of the hills, every new valley - and many enormous crags.

At each stop he gathered up the folds of his anorak, to squeeze pints of rainwater from the bottom edge, where the drawstring seemed to perform like a sponge. Not that it mattered much at this stage anyway, as his trousers were wringing wet, and clung like soggy blankets around his cold legs.

He was aware that the cloud base was lowering rapidly as the rain became more persistent.

Ten minutes later he looked back, to see the cloud still fifty feet behind him, and catching up fast.

Another ten minutes passed. The rain drummed on his hood like a waterfall, and the path beneath his feet was rapidly turning into a stream. He had given up trying to squeeze excess water from his clothing. Every time he shook out the water, it was quickly replenished, and he could feel his toes beginning to wrinkle inside his socks.

Reaching the car was something close to ecstasy. His change of clothes was warm and dry, and there was a whole flask of hot coffee waiting in the boot. It took several minutes to peel off each wet layer, rub himself on a towel, and put on the dry set. Standing there in his underpants, he smiled as he realised there wasn't another soul around for miles.

Just the ducks!

The following day was a complete contrast. The sun broke over the rim of the mountains on the first light of morning, and shone warmly through the afternoon as if to make amends for its disgraceful conduct of the previous day.

Roy found himself drawn to the sharp ridges which make up the High Stile range, seen in silhouette from the lakeside as a line of dramatic crags. By coffee time he was half way up the blind valley of Burtness Comb, looking for a safe way onto the ridge.

There was no obvious path in the bracken and scree, and the way ahead was barred by an insurmountable wall, sheer and high, known as Eagle Crag. Lit by the morning sun, it looked a friendly crag, although completely out of bounds for the likes of Roy. It is no wonder that the eagles, those beautiful birds which gave their name to the crag, should choose such places for the site of their nests.

Unfortunately the mountains in this area are now just a bit too busy for eagles, and none have nested there for some years.

High crags surrounded Roy as he made his way upwards. Looking to his left he noticed a sloping gully of scree running up between two outcrops. Could this be what he was looking for?

"Sheepbone Rake," he announced to himself, recognising the gully as the recommended route in the Wainwright book.

It was one of the few breaches in the line of crags, and from where Roy stood, it looked a safe bet for a quick way onto the topmost ridges.

He paused for a few minutes, looking at the quantities of rubble that had come down the chute over the years, and reflected on the name - "rake" - often found in guide books, describing an easy gully.

In fact, the name seems to refer to any easy passage between two crags, or through areas which are otherwise inaccessible. The dictionary is not very explicit. The nearest Roy could find was a reference to "incline from the perpendicular," which seemed to fit fairly accurately.

Reaching the foot of the Rake, he was already on loose scree, and could see lumps of rock and gravel stretching out above him, all the way up to the horizon.

It was steep enough to test his expertise on scree, and he was soon fighting to remain upright as he dislodged huge quantities of debris.

Flailing his arms like a windmill, he struggled to the side of the chute, where he could hang on to some firm rock for a few moments.

"Hold on," he told himself. "Slow down a bit!"

The solution was found. He slowed to a rhythmic plod, and for the most part, prevented any further rockslides.

Buttermere

This "easy" way up the crag tested the legs, the joints, the balance and the nerves, but as a spectacle it was a little disappointing. There was no sense of exposure, no feeling of being on the edge of a crag, just a close-up view of small boulders and loose gravel stretching from his feet, up to the skyline as far as he could see.

The joy was soon to come. On reaching the solid rock shoulder at the top of the gully, he was rewarded with a terrific view over Buttermere, and realised that he was virtually on top of the world. The rough track led on from there to the summit of the crag in a short series of simple scrambles.

He suddenly felt that the day was getting rather hot, and stripped off down to his cotton shirt, stuffing his anorak and pullover into the rucksack.

It was a truly wonderful day to be out on the fell-tops, and looking down, he enjoyed the spectacle of Eagle Crag, plunging in a long vertical drop to the stony bed of Burtness Comb.

Roy looked with great interest at the Comb, a dry valley littered with loose rock - obviously the remains of rock-falls from the crag itself.

His path led along the rim of the crag, and he felt a tremendous degree of exposure as he skirted the edge, enjoying the unrivalled views of Buttermere, some 2500 feet below.

He turned around, and suddenly realised that he could see into the adjacent valley of Ennerdale. Gentle slopes led down to the forestry plantations which are a feature of this green valley, and just across the other side, the crags of Pillar and Steeple made a dramatic silhouette against the sunlit sky.

But it was the view over Buttermere that held him in awe. The world below was transformed into a map, Nothing seemed to move, except the occasional ripple on the surface of the lake, or the flash of light reflected from the windscreen of an unseen car, moving slowly along a faint brown line in the valley bottom.

The mountains across the other side were huge - even larger than they looked from the lakeside.

Their names were straight from the yellow pages - Robinson, Hindscarth and Dalehead, and Roy remembered reading somewhere that these three summits were referred to as "the solicitors."

"They're nothing like solicitors," he thought. "They look large, sleek and friendly." The last solicitor Roy had seen was short, bespectacled and definitely not the outdoor type.

Robinson, in particular, looked massive, and shimmered in the haze of the afternoon sun, painted in delicate pastel shades from green to purple.

Feeling rather dehydrated, he removed his pack, and collapsed onto a rock, letting his rucksack go like a ton of bricks onto the floor.

"This is ridiculous," he thought as he searched for his flask amongst the contents of the sack. "I've got everything but the kitchen sink in here."

It was packed almost to bursting point with waterproofs, lunch, discarded anorak, pullover, first aid, photographic equipment (including tripod), maps, guide book, chocolate, fruit, water bottle, flask of tea and survival bag.

"Serves you right," he told himself, wiping the perspiration from his face. "You don't need half this stuff today."

It's a dilemma which confronts every mountaineer, what to carry on the day. Take too much, and it makes hard work. Leave anything behind, and you're sure to want it. Forget the waterproofs, and it is bound to rain!

To be realistic, at the end of the day it's probably the most prepared walker who emerges unscathed. You never know what the weather is going to do in this typically British climate.

But for everyone there is the ultimate reward waiting at the end of the walk.

No matter how dehydrated you are, how many blisters you have accumulated, or whether your knees have become swollen, once the load has been deposited in the boot of the car the next stop is the village shop, where you can find drinks, fruit, yoghurts, hot meals and relaxation.

Just around the corner is the local pub, where the hardened mountaineers congregate to exchange stories, sitting at the outside tables with their enormous rucksacks standing beside them. The bigger the rucksack, the better the story of conquest, ordeal and endeavour!

The Heatwave

Boy, was it hot! Roy was faced with a simple choice.... He would wander down to the local pub and cool off with a litre or two of lager. But then a more compelling thought flooded his mind - visions of cooling breezes on a sunny mountain top. The pub would have to wait.

All parts of the British Isles were enjoying a long hot summer like they had never known before, and Roy arrived in Ambleside at a time when the grass was dying, and cracks were appearing twelve inches deep in the fields. Local farmers were contemplating suicide as their crops failed.

It was a rare opportunity to indulge in a photographic week, in the knowledge that there would be no rain, no gales, no snow, and no fog!

The plan was to walk up Loughrigg on the first day, a simple climb of a thousand feet or so, to stretch his legs. Later in the week, with the certainty of long sunny days ahead of him, he would explore some of the higher fells around Ambleside and Grasmere.

The sun was high in the sky when he arrived at the foot of Loughrigg, and parked the car in the shade of some tall pines alongside the road. The local radio station announced "temperatures in the eighties, and a high risk of fire on the open moors."

It all sounded too much. He reached for the canister of water, which had started off that morning cool and refreshing, but during the course of the journey it had turned into a disgusting luke-warm liquid. Nevertheless, he drank about a pint of it before embarking on the walk.

The first stretch was easy - up a leafy lane beneath oak, sycamore and horse chestnut. "This is very pleasant," he thought. "Just what the doctor ordered."

As he progressed slowly up the track, the humidity became almost unbearable. It was like a steam bath in the woods, and a strong smell of cow-dung wafted gently across from the adjacent farm.

There was a constant buzz of insects as they revelled in the tropical conditions. Just ahead, in the clearings, he could see the air thick with flies, spinning round in the shafts of sunlight percolating through the leaf canopy.

Flies - he hated them!

Last week had been the limit. He'd walked through a plague of Scottish midges, bitten all over, and finished up with arms and legs the size of footballs. Then he had to endure the ultimate indignity of a penicillin jab in his rear quarters. All very painful.

"Never again," he vowed.

Yet here they were, hundreds of them. Very soon the air was thick with the little monsters, and they homed in on him as he quickened his pace.

"Gerroff you little perishers!" he cursed, waving the map at them. "Where's my repellant spray?"

It was no good looking for the spray - it wasn't there. In fact it was about a hundred miles away, locked in his bathroom.

On reaching the ridge, there was some respite from the insects, and the heat seemed less intense with the slight movement of air.

"Definitely over 80," he decided. "Probably 85 down in the valley.

The map indicated a little tarn just over the ridge, and the refreshing thought prompted him to look for it. In a shallow depression he found a boggy area containing tall reeds and cotton grass. Then he found a small swamp, only a few yards across, now no more than a puddle of smelly brown mud. If this has been a tarn, it must have dried up in the heat!

He spent a few minutes chasing some orange moths, trying to photograph them, but they were too quick. Then he noticed scores of blue damsel flies flitting here and there over the damp grass. These were even quicker.

The Heatwave

The moment the horse-flies swarmed in, Roy was off again, heading for the highest point of the fell. Having reached it, he collapsed onto a rock and measured out the remains of his water supply - luke-warm tea in the bottom of the flask.

In the relentless sunshine, his arms were already beginning to get the red luminous look - and this was only the first day!

Returning along the ridge, he circled round a group of rocks and stumbled upon the tarn - the *real* tarn - a pool of rippling water, the one he was looking for earlier in the day. It all looked cool and refreshing, especially the white water-lillies in full bloom around the edges.

He felt the water. It was quite warm, despite its depth. What a glorious relief to splash quantities of it over his head and shoulders. His sunburn almost sizzled as the water evaporated.

Returning to the car, it was good to see that the shady trees had kept it reasonably cool, and he settled into the driving seat with a long satisfying drink in his hand - perfect bliss!

The following day dawned clear and sunny again, and the met men were forecasting another scorcher, with temperatures approaching 90!

It was a great temptation to take a day off and see the mountains from the comfort of a shady table in the village. However, Roy had planned a fairly short walk from Grasmere, aiming for Easedale Tarn and the dramatic peak of Sergeant Man. This walk was very popular with the tourists - there were crowds of them already heading up the track.

Before setting off, he spent some time trying to ensure that the car, parked in the open sun, would not heat up like an oven. He stuck newspapers against the windscreen and side windows until every bit of glass was covered. It looked good, but how effective would it be?

At ten o'clock the heat of the day was already building up. The sky was a continuous blue, and the sun had a feeling of relentless scorching aggression.

Leaving Grasmere behind, Roy could pick out the well-worn route ahead. He recognised Sourmilk Gill, tumbling down the hillside in a series of rapids, which made the water appear milky.

"Yes - Sourmilk!"

The track wound its way alongside the Gill, heading uphill towards Easedale Tarn, hidden somewhere over the brink of a hanging valley a thousand feet above him.

He caught up with several groups of walkers picking their way slowly up the path, and wondered how far everyone would get on a day like this. It was suicidal!

There were small groups of trees at intervals alongside the stream, and Roy was pleased to find that the shady hollows were still relatively cool under the canopy of leaves. Unfortunately the supply of trees ran out as he gained height. It was open moorland from there on, and no shade at all.

He soon caught up with a party of about thirty school children, accompanied by half a dozen teachers. Some of the teachers were already having a hard time of it, trying to shepherd their classes in an orderly fashion, but they were soon to find that on a mountain walk, discipline is very hard to enforce, and some members were always streets ahead of the rest.

The youngsters were mostly in the 8 to 10 age group, very young for such a walk, but were generally well behaved, spending their time chasing dragon flies or plucking handfuls of cotton grass to decorate their collars and trouser belts.

One of the back-markers was a deformed girl, short and chubby, about two-foot-six in height, her little bowed legs striding out purposely as she chased after the rest of the party. She had already climbed about six hundred feet and kept on without a rest, despite the obvious effort needed to keep up the pace. Roy took his hat off to her. It was good to see her enjoying the walk.

He kept a fairly slow pace just in front of the school party, watching the cool water of the Gill as it bounced on its rocky course only a few yards from the path. It had a refreshing effect, and helped to ease the pain of the gradient for the last two hundred feet. The path gradually levelled out over the last ridge into the hanging valley, and there before him was Easedale Tarn, cool and level, its great expanse rippling gently in the slight breeze.

The Heatwave

Sparkling flashes of sunlight reflected from every ripple, and the feeling of peace and tranquility made him pause for a few minutes.

The school party arrived over the rim of the valley, settling down near the tarn on a grassy bank. One of the masters started telling them about glaciers, and how the retreating ice left a moraine, a block of rocks which held back the waters of Easedale Tarn.

It was all good stuff, and very interesting, but Roy hadn't come all this way for a geography lesson. Continuing on his way, he could trace his intended path rising through a gap in the hills and disappearing into a second valley, a little higher than the first.

Here he found Codale Tarn, a small lake lying in a green basin, looking as though it had been undisturbed for centuries. The silence was a complete contrast to the hustle and bustle of Easedale.

Pale blue damsel flies mingled with the Common Blue and Small Copper butterflies around his feet. Then two distinct breeds of fly began to show interest in Roy's arms and neck, already well patterned with red dots and blotches from the day before.

He departed quickly from the idyllic valley and headed for the ridge which would lead him to Sergeant Man.

He had set off with a plentiful supply of liquids. This included a four-pint milk carton filled with water, stuffed into his rucksack along with all the other gear he always carried. The weight was unbelievable, and his shoulders felt as though he had been carrying a piano. But it was proving to be worth it as he enjoyed the luxury of a drink, just when he was feeling very dehydrated.

The mountains flanking the Codale basin were the highest part of his walk, and Roy tried to find new energy as he recognised the conical peak of Sergeant Man peeping over the rim of the valley. There seemed to be a swirling haze over the peak, making it look like a false image, or mirage. The surrounding hills, too, were swaying, like the movement of an ocean. He blinked and looked again. The hills shimmered and flickered.

"Keep still a minute!" Roy grunted, falling heavily against a rock.

Then he realised it wasn't the mountains that were moving, it was the illusion of his own eyes, his senses, and his balance. He felt sick.

The day was getting far too hot for expeditions like this. He should have stayed by the lakeside with the geography classes!

He searched the sky for any sign of clouds. There was nothing but deep blue from one end to the other, and the fiery orb of the sun, suspended right over his head, relentless.... torturing.....

With some effort Roy straightened himself, and plodded on up the path. He thought of the cool water of Easedale Tarn sparkling in the sun, and allowed his mind to wander through the cafes of Grasmere. He dreamed about cool dishes of ice-cream, and imagined a glass of shandy, foaming over as he raised it to his lips.

He snapped back to reality as he stumbled over a small outcrop of rock, and sat on it for a few seconds, looking around him. His hands ran nervously through his hair, which felt as though it was on fire.

"Everything's so dry," he thought. It was relentless, a yellow, parched landscape - in every direction.

A few minutes later, as he plodded over the next rise, the bulk of Sergeant Man came into full view, about half a mile away, the summit perched on top of a craggy hill.

Several walkers already shared the rocky platform. They'd obviously set off far earlier than Roy had!

He arrived at the base of the final hill almost on bended knees, heart pounding, head throbbing, eyes bulging and throat parched, and realised that he was feeling the heat very badly that day.

He picked a zig-zag course, staggering slowly - ever more slowly - sometimes almost stopping.

Lifting his head occasionally, he felt he was making no progress at all. He wasn't getting any closer.

The summit shimmered and swayed, and Roy felt himself staggering into the heather at the side of the track.

"Must be a touch of heat-stroke!"

He grew hotter and hotter until his head felt as though it would burst. His shirt was wet through with perspiration, and his skin felt to be frying in the sun. His hair was like an electric hotplate, burning his scalp, and both arms were tingling as they assumed an even brighter red.

55

The Heatwave

At long last Roy managed to haul himself, stone by stone, up to the summit, and his legs folded under him as he reached the cairn.

He was alone - the previous group of walkers had already gone on their way. His face felt the impact of sharp stones as he hit the floor.

His stomach lurched, and as he lay in a semi-dead position, he shivered.

He remained motionless for some time, clutching at the base of the cairn for the reassurance that his climb was over. The ground stopped moving.

No more toiling - no more suicidal ascents!

The breeze began to cool his body temperature, and within a few minutes he noticed he wasn't sweating any more.

As time passed, he felt strength running back into his limbs, and suddenly realised he was hungry. That was a good sign - he wasn't going to die after all.

Sorting through his rucksack, he took out all the food he had specially selected for the walk - things that were wet and sweet, like jam, fruit, tinned pears, swiss rolls and yoghurt. These high-energy foods, together with lots of liquids, quickly refreshed him.

The route downhill was delightfully easy, and he wondered what all the fuss had been about, but once below the rim of the valley, the hot air met him again. The afternoon was noticeably hotter than the morning had been.

Large flies attacked in even greater numbers, driven mad at the sight of humans perspiring in the sun.

Roy frantically waved the map at them, but failed to discourage their persistence, although the wafting action did create a little air movement around his ears.

Descending from the Codale basin down the rocky stream course, the bouncing, bubbling water became too much of a temptation. Roy climbed down to the water level and splashed all his sunburnt areas with cool, refreshing water. Then, seeing a small waterfall, he stuck his head and shoulders completely under the falling torrent, drenching himself to the waist. It was bliss - a joy to end all joys!

Searching in his sack, he found a large rag that had once been a cotton shirt, and soaked it in the stream. It was wonderfully cool to the head, and the back of his neck, just the thing for a day like this.

As he walked past Easedale Tarn, he soaked the rag again, repeating the treatment at every opportunity. It was the answer to his problems, and for the rest of the walk he managed to stay relatively cool and fresh.

On reaching the car, he found the door handle too hot to touch. When he did manage to open it, a blast of sickly hot air met him.

The thermometer registered 155 degrees, and there was no way he was going to get inside until it cooled off.

So much for the newspapers! He locked the car up, and headed off down to the pub for that glass of shandy.

BUTTERMERE FACTFILE

Buttermere -
twin lakes, Buttermere and Crummock Water
Fell walks -
Whiteless Pike - 2159 ft.   Easy
Robinson - 2417 ft.   Easy/Moderate
High Stile - 2644 ft.   Moderate
Access Roads - Honister Pass - Cockermouth

LOUGHRIGG / SERGEANT MAN

Loughrigg - 1101 ft.   Easy
Nearest town - Ambleside
Features - Loughrigg Tarn

Sergeant Man - 2414 ft.   Easy
Nearest town - Grasmere
Features - Easedale Tarn, Codale Tarn

Holme Moss

Holme Moss is probably known to most people as the name of a regional television transmitter in West Yorkshire. It actually stands on the boundary between Yorkshire and Derbyshire.

The mast itself is a dominant feature, standing hundreds of feet high, visible for many miles in every direction.

Local walkers, however, know this more intimately as an outstanding moorland area, part of the Pennine Chain. There are great opportunities here for outdoor pursuits, especially on the wild hill-tops, where one can find a unique collection of eroded peat bogs, a landscape so inhospitable and barren that it might have come from the mountains of the moon. Yet on a good day the moor can be warm, colourful and friendly.

During a particularly cold spell in mid-February, Roy looked at his map and decided that the Holme Moss area would be ideal for a club walk. He was responsible for planning and organisation within the works social club, and felt that it was time they got away from their desks and did some real work on the moors!

There was plenty of snow about, bringing the usual disruption to road and rail services. Furthermore, he knew that if the towns were frozen into Winter, then logically the hilltops might be worse, probably too inhospitable for the regular walkers of the club. So he had to go and reconnoitre, to see for himself what the conditions were like up there.

He was pleased to find that Dave had booked the same day off, and thought it might be prudent to get a second opinion before committing the club members to the walk. Not everyone would relish going on the moors in snow, but there were many of them who would jump at the chance.

It hadn't snowed for two days, so the roads were clear, and there was no problem getting to Holme Moss.

The usual car park near the transmitter was completely snowbound, but it was easy enough to park at the side of the road where the snowploughs had been.

The sun shone strongly from a blue sky, but the temperature must have been several degrees below freezing, with a fresh northerly wind making it feel desperately cold.

Roy and Dave prepared themselves for some hard walking, putting on waterproof outfits for extra protection.

Leaving the safety of the road, they ploughed straight into deep snow, hard and crusty on top, but soft and powdery underneath.

"I've got four layers of wool under my anorak," Dave announced. "I feel like an eskimo."

"You look like one," Roy assured him. "It's the red nose that gives you away!"

Fifty yards from the road, heading for the heart of the moor, they were already experiencing great difficulty in the arctic conditions. The snow depth varied from one foot to three feet or more, and it was virtually impossible to detect what pitfalls lay below the snow cover. The moor itself is an area of dunes, peat bog and natural ditches, but under the February snow all the features were lost.

After half an hour of this rough walking, Roy stopped and leaned on his stick.

"Hang on a minute," he called, "I'm ready for a rest!"

Dave turned round. His face was red, and he could hardly find enough breath to speak. He simply allowed himself to collapse into the snow, and they sat together recovering with chocolate biscuits and a flask of tea.

There were several stops during the next hour, due to the high work-rate needed to raise each foot out of the snow - like going uphill all the time.

Holme Moss

The hollows and ditches were completely hidden under a flat layer of snow. One moment Roy and Dave were making good progress in a foot of firm snow, then in one stride they were up to their waists in it. Half a dozen floundering steps, and they found firm ground again. Again they stopped to gasp for breath, leaning with their hands on their knees, panting loudly.

They occasionally took time out to admire the scenery. In the unbroken sunshine it looked like Switzerland. The curved snowdrifts, sometimes towering to eight feet or more, were like dazzling waves frozen in time, sparkling like icing sugar in the brightness of the sun.

With every turn, there were more breathtaking arrays of drifts, all blown the same way, sculptured by the wind into fantastic curves and waves.

What a feast of photography! The cameras were out almost constantly. Roy found himself searching for words which were adequate for the situation, and having found one, spoke it aloud, as if addressing the snowdrifts themselves. "Great!" "Fantastic!" "Oh boy!"

During one of their stops, they spent some time tracing the tracks of hares. The prints were everywhere, tracking across the snow, running up and over the drifts, criss-crossing and turning in circles. There were play areas where the tracks were merged into a mass of trodden snow, and plenty of evidence of where hares go to relieve themselves!

In the lee of some long, high dunes, Roy and Dave spread out some waterproof sheets and took their lunch sitting in the warm rays of the afternoon sun. They thoroughly enjoyed the comparative warmth of their sheltered position, knowing that only ten feet away over the drifts the wind was howling at near gale force, and the temperature out there was still below freezing.

Dave used his knife to peel the accumulated ice from his trousers and socks, which had become so encrusted that they must have weighed double.

Twenty minutes later, they began to feel the cold penetrating the waterproof sheets, and were forced into action, packing their rucksacks and retracing their steps towards the television mast and the car.

"The wind's getting stronger," Roy remarked, hooding up tightly.

"Yeah, right in our faces," Dave replied, showing the redness in his frozen cheeks as he spoke.

Roy's face, too, was red and quite numb. It had been a long time since he last had any feeling in his nose, and his ears were smarting.

He was intrigued to see the relentless creeping carpet of loose ice particles flowing over his boots. The wind kept the crystals moving, spinning, whispering, then picked them up, hurled them in his face, cutting like sandpaper.

All trace of footprints had been wiped out by the wind-storm, and Roy had to make a new route through the drifts. Plunging through virgin snow again seemed even harder on this return leg. But at least the extra energy had the effect of warming up chilled bodies, and restoring the circulation, which had suffered somewhat over lunch.

The tall mast seemed nearer, and soon they were walking past the ice-encrusted stay-wires which support the structure. The build-up of ice was unbelievable. In places it was hanging off in lumps six feet long.

Dave remarked that it was similar to the old mast on Emley Moor, which had collapsed several years ago under the weight of ice. It was not the place to hang around too long. Indeed there were notices to the public, warning everyone to keep clear. Roy and Dave needed no further prompting.

They stumbled out of the snow onto the road, and ran over to the car. It was warm and comfortable inside. The effect of sunshine through the windscreen made it rather like a greenhouse. It took them a few minutes to locate their bootlaces under the thick layer of ice. The boots themselves weighed a ton, and it was sheer luxury to change into some trainers.

"What do you think then?" Roy prompted. "Will the members like it?"

Dave nodded. "Yes, I think so."

"Next Sunday then!"

So it was all fixed.

It snowed again during the week, and most of the high roads were closed again. Reports on the radio became more depressing as the week went on, and it looked as though the club walk might have to be cancelled.

Roy was determined to make the best of the situation, and called a meeting of all the prospective walkers.

Holme Moss

Surprisingly there was general agreement, and an optimistic feeling amongst the members. They would walk, whatever the weather. Little did they know what they were letting themselves in for!

Sunday morning came, and the snowstorm had abated, apart from the odd flurry from the east. The snowploughs had been out, and most roads were fairly good, although some of the housing estates were still isolated because of the ungritted surface.

Two full cars arrived in Holme village, carrying seven members of the works social club. Originally it had been a large party of sixteen, but most of them had chickened out, and were probably still in bed.

"Sheer madness," one had said.

"You're off your rockers," said the boss.

"You don't know what you're missing," Roy replied. He was right!

On reaching the village, they discovered that the road was closed ahead, and if they wanted to go any further it would have to be on foot.

"OK," said Derek, one of the regulars. "Let's park here and get on our way."

By mid-morning they were fully prepared, dressed in an assortment of arctic walking gear, and set off up the road towards the television mast. They couldn't see it, but knew it was up there somewhere!

To make matters worse, the snow started again, and all the surrounding hilltops were completely hidden in thick cloud.

What horrors awaited the party? What would the conditions be like up there?

Leaving Holme village, the main discomfort was the easterly wind, howling over the white fields and spreading blizzard-like clouds over the stone walls. A sea of whirling snow crystals poured onto the road like a tidal wave. In many places the walls themselves had vanished. Parked cars were completely snowed over, appearing as white mounds. Sometimes the corner of a roof would identify the drift as a buried vehicle.

The road had been cleared that morning, and presented fairly easy walking, but outside the village the party soon found hard-packed snow underfoot, rutted into narrow tracks left by the farmers in their tractors.

One such tractor passed them, forcing them to leap into the snowdrifts at the side of the road. The farmer looked out of his cab.

"You're all mad!" he shouted.

"No problems," Roy replied, stumbling into deep snow.

About half-way up the winding road, Roy called the party to a halt.

"We'd better not leave the road today," he advised. "We'd never find it again."

Everyone agreed. Visibility was very poor, and the road was already beginning to look as bad as the surrounding fields. It was a good half hour since they last saw a farm, a vehicle or anything else, and there was no traffic to prevent the road from covering over in long white drifts.

The biting wind lashed against their backs, but thanks to their heavy waterproofs and the thick layers of wool underneath, they felt comfortable enough.

Roy was very conscious of his responsibility towards the rest of the party, and felt pleased that everything was going well, but it had crossed his mind that it wouldn't be quite so comfortable coming back on the return journey. Every time he turned round to check that they were still with him, he got a face-full of snow crystals, biting his cheeks and piercing his eyes. He decided to forget the return journey for the time being, and concentrated on navigating uphill.

He sensed that they were getting fairly close to the top, but couldn't see a thing in front of him. The drifts were getting deeper, and he could see the huge curved snowdrifts on the moor growing larger and larger by the minute. In the gale-force wind they were marching towards the road, building higher as they approached.

On reaching the road, the drifts simply continued building, reaching across until they joined with those on the other side, forming a continuous barrier.

Only the marker posts remained to show where the road was. What a blessing. Without them, there would have been no clue, and the party might have wandered off, never to be seen again!

Holme Moss

"Everyone OK?" Roy enquired, looking to see if the back-markers were catching up.

"Yes, OK," Derek replied. "Just a bit worried about Jill, she's only got short legs, you know."

Jill was doing fine. Following on at the back, she was ploughing through the gaps made by the rest of the party, and although she was only five feet in height, it didn't deter her.

Derek was walking well, always up at the front with Roy, giving moral support.

"I'll let you lead for a bit," Roy suggested.

"No, after you," Derek replied. "You're the only one who knows where we're going!"

Roy continued, striding uphill. The snow was very fine and powdery, and when he kicked through a drift, it exploded in a shower of ice particles, to be picked up in the wind and blown away. Then, as Derek and the others followed through the gap, the snow began to drift back, building again until nobody could see where the gap had been.

They were desperately trying not to lose the road, trying to keep a straight course for the next marker.

The moor was a land of grotesque sculptures carved in white. Huge, tall, curving shapes, towering to eight feet, in a constant state of movement, reshaping, building and remodelling.

The shapes seemed to be alive, conspiring to dominate, to overpower, to bar the way completely. Making progress required sustained effort, hacking through, only to find more of them, taller, thicker and deeper.

"Hang on a minute," Derek called, "We've lost Jill."

"No you haven't," came a little voice from the back. "That last one collapsed on me."

Jill strode into view, white from head to foot, scooping snow out of her collar and spitting it out of her mouth.

"The abominable snowman!" shouted Cliff, who was supposed to have been watching her.

"Just take a look at yourself," she retorted. A valid remark! Everyone was almost completely white, difficult to recognise one person from another. Icicles hung from the corners of anoraks, and mushy snow caked on eyebrows and moustaches.

Derek suggested a stop somewhere, but there was nowhere that seemed to offer any shelter at all. The atmosphere was a swirling whiteness, and the wind seemed to come from every direction at once.

Then Roy spotted what he had been looking for, a line of road markers running off to the right. He might easily have missed them, but during a short lull, the snow stopped spinning for a second, and the markers came into view.

"Holme Moss transmitter station!" he shouted, pointing along the line of posts, and started following them. This was the access road. Could there be shelter ahead?

After a few minutes floundering through deep snow they were delighted to see the wire netting enclosure and the big double gates of the transmitter station. And there, just above them, the base of the mast.

They had made it. The gates were open, but there was no sign of life. Inside the compound the snow had accumulated to a level six feet, and it was clearly impossible to progress any further towards the buildings. In any case, there wasn't any sign of life, no lights, no smoking chimneys.... nothing!

There was no natural shelter at all, and the wind buffeted across in gusts of around force ten. Snow blew horizontally in hard, piercing crystals and the cold was beginning to penetrate through their waterproofs.

It was a stroke of good fortune that left a hollow just inside the gates, where the spinning wind had whipped up the snow and cleared it down to road level. There was just room for the seven of them to huddle together, standing, surrounded by walls of white, eight feet high. Out came the flasks of soup and tea. bars of chocolate, and all the good things they had been looking forward to.

There was just time for a quick photograph, then they had to fasten up the rucksacks which had begun to fill up with snow. It was getting into everything - every chink in their clothing, down their necks and even through the button holes.

There was no time to lose - they must get down to civilisation before they froze to death.

Leaving the shelter of the hollow was the most uncomfortable part of the journey so far. The wind hit

Holme Moss

them the moment they emerged, causing them to stumble from the track as they fought their way back to the road. They could see nothing apart from the marker posts, and even then they could only look five yards ahead because of the snow crystals, stabbing like needles into their faces and eyes.

Roy paused for a moment. He had lost the markers. He knew he was somewhere near the road, and could not take the risk of missing it. There was nothing but open moorland all around, with unpredictable pitfalls like cliffs and quarries. He must find the road.

Then Derek spotted another marker, some way to the left. Beyond it was a second marker, then a third.

Yes, it was definitely the road. They lost no time following the posts and were relieved to find that they were heading downhill.

Fifty yards further, they hit the spindrift at the top of the steep section, where the wind was funnelled by the contours into something approaching a hurricane. There was no trace of earlier footprints, and the gaps which they had made in the drifts were all snowed up again. The route was hardly recognisable in the swirling snow, and the air was so thick they could hardly see their own feet, or the person standing next to them.

They stood for a minute as the wind suddenly gusted, lifting tons of snow into the air and whirling it round in an inpenetrable blanket.

"Hell, I can't see a thing," Roy cursed, trying to keep the snow out of his eyes, but whichever way he looked the wind was blowing the stuff into his face. Even with his head down he couldn't see his boots. It was a complete white-out. There was nothing he could do but stand there, trying to keep upright in the tearing wind.

The gale eased for a second, they staggered to the next marker, and stood again until they could see ahead.

Cliff broke the tension with a nervous laugh. "Just look at yourselves," he chuckled, "You look like a bunch of snowmen."

"At least there's still seven of us," Roy remarked, thankfully. "We haven't managed to lose anybody."

Half an hour later they noticed a definite lull in the wind. The conditions improved considerably as they cut their way through the snow, still following the marker posts.

Soon they were passing the point where they had seen the farmer earlier in the day.

"Civilisation!" shouted Derek, waving his fist in the air in a gesture of triumph.

There were no more snowdrifts, no more wallowing through it, just hard-packed snow on the road.

As they neared the village they walked onto level tarmac once more. One or two tourists had gathered to watch. They'd never seen eskimoes before.

"Last one in the pub pays!" Derek shouted, setting off like a hare towards the inn where they had parked the cars.

Roy began to wonder about the remark the farmer had thrown at them. Were they all mad? Or were they to be congratulated on a smart bit of survival work?

As they sat in the pub, steaming in front of an open fire, glass in hand, they felt a glow in their bodies, the blood surging through their feet, and a feeling of elation over their survival.

The barman was very impressed. He had to be. Trade had been very slack recently. Today was his lucky day!

HOLME MOSS FACTFILE

Holme Moss - 1908 ft.   Easy
Nearest towns - Huddersfield, Holmfirth
Features - Television tranmitter mast
Eroded peat moorland
The Pennine Way - long distance path

Robinson

Robinson, overlooking Buttermere Lake, completely dominates the surrounding fells, calling out a challenge to all walkers who are lucky enough to visit this lovely valley.

Roy and Dave's explorations in this area resulted in the discovery of a delightful circular walk, a thrilling scramble encompassing the peaks of Robinson and Hindscarth, with outstanding views over Buttermere.

It hadn't been easy. Some of the early climbs were long and arduous, but the final discovery of the 7-mile circular made it all worth while.

It all began over a beer-stained table in a typical public house somewhere in Yorkshire. Roy and Dave planned all their walks this way. Somehow the genial surroundings made it easier to talk.

"How about Robinson?" suggested Dave.
"Jack Robinson?"
"No, the mountain."
"A bit steep," Roy observed. "Can we find an easier one?"
"Straight up from Buttermere," Dave insisted. "It's a doddle."
"I'd rather try it from the other side," Roy argued. "Catbells looks a better approach."
"But that's too long. You're looking at a twelve mile walk."
"Yes, but it's not as steep," Roy explained, and Dave had to agree.
"You know what you are," Dave said. "You're basically lazy, unfit - a disgrace!"
Roy nodded. "OK, I'll let you try it first, and I'll wait in the car."
Dave thought for a minute.
"Would you like me to organise a helicopter for you?"
"Now you're talking!"

So it was to be Catbells! Starting near Keswick, they parked the car in a small layby overlooking Derwentwater. Half an hour of scrambling saw them onto the ridge, where they could look along the line of crags and see what they had to do.

It looked simple enough. The ridge ran south towards Honister, over a succession of tops, each one higher than the last. Then the path turned up Dale Head, over Hindscarth and on to Robinson.

It was clearly going to be a full day's walk, but Roy felt that it was well within their reach. They would be back by teatime.

A nice grassy track led up onto Maiden Moor, the next high point, then another simple ridge to High Spy, only 300 feet higher.

It was going very well, and they weren't even panting!

"See, I told you, didn't I?" Roy grinned. Dave chose to ignore the remark, but he too was clearly enjoying the relaxed start to the walk.

After a few minutes they caught up with a small group of middle-aged walkers, two men and two women. They were suitably clad, with boots, anoraks and small rucksacks, and the men seemed to be enjoying it. Their wives, however, were struggling.

"Albert!" called the slim one. "Just wait a minute!"
Albert either didn't hear, or wasn't listening, and was fast disappearing round the next outcrop.
"Albert!" - no reply.

The plumper woman was just collapsing onto a rock, her face contorted with the effort, becoming bright red, especially her ears, and perspiration poured from her chin.

"Mary, I can't go on," she called to her companion. "I wish they'd wait for us."

She was no spring chicken, and clearly felt the effects of the climb more than the others. She groaned loudly, and moaned so fearfully, it sounded like her last breath on this earth.

Dave made sure they were going to survive, and promised to stop Albert before he got too far ahead. He turned to Roy. "Typical! The men race off, and the women have to sort themselves out."

Five minutes later, they saw Albert and his friend walking back to find the girls. Roy and Dave continued up the ridge.

"This is High Spy," Roy shouted, as he gained the small cairn.

"Yes, we're over 2000 feet now," Dave added, looking at the map. "But it's funny, it's clearly marked Eel Crags, not High Spy."

Roy looked puzzled for a moment. They had climbed Eel Crags the day before, but it definitely wasn't on this ridge. Those crags had been about four miles to the north.

"Must be two of them," he suggested.

"Might be more than two," Dave added. "It's a bit like Grisedale and Blea Tarn. There's dozens of them, all with the same name."

It didn't help the confusion, but Roy felt a lot better knowing that it wasn't his navigation that had gone wrong.

Robinson was clearly visible to the west. Only two peaks separated them from their goal, Dale Head and Hindscarth.

There was a slight dip in the ridge, where the quiet water of a tarn made it an ideal spot for coffee. Looking at Dale Head from here, it was a daunting prospect. The track turned upwards towards the sky, continuing steeply into the clouds until it ran out of sight.

It was as severe as anything they had encountered that week. In fact it might have been worse than Robinson itself!

"We've failed!" Roy remarked in some dispair. "We might have been better going the short way from Buttermere!"

"And saved about eight miles of walking," Dave added.

It was 800 feet of unrelenting slog, and seemed to go on forever, but eventually it eased off, and the summit of Dale Head came into view.

The cairn was a masterpiece. Constructed securely in flat stone, it looked strong enough to withstand anything the weather could throw at it, including rain, snow and gales. Its neat appearance is unusual in that it stands on a narrow base and bulges in the middle.

They finally reached Robinson at lunchtime. Well, to be exact, 2.30 was lunchtime that day. Time didn't seem to matter very much up there, and anyway, as Dave pointed out, the sheep didn't stick to any set times, and they looked healthy enough.

This arrangement seemed to suit Dave and Roy. It was not unusual for them to have three lunchtimes in one day!

Robinson had nothing dramatic around its summit, just a rough cairn, but the views were superb, and the blue water of Buttermere gleamed in the afternoon sunlight, so warm and inviting.

"You know, we've slipped up here," Roy remarked. "Do you realise we have to go back over Dale Head again?"

"Yes, I'd thought of that," Dave nodded. "We should have left the car in Newlands, then we could run straight down from here."

"We'll try that next time," suggested Roy.

"What next time?"

From Dale Head they took the old miners' track down to the valley, and left themselves a simple low-level walk back to the car.

About half-way home, they passed through several slate tips which marked the location of old copper mines. Some of the horizontal workings were still there as dark forbidding holes in the mountain side, whilst other openings had been partly hidden under tons of slate.

Roy wandered off to look at the old buildings, their roofs long since gone and the walls crumbling away under the effects of the weather.

"Hey, look at this!" he called, and Dave ran over to see what treasure he had uncovered.

"Slates - with messages!"

"They're all girls," Roy observed.

"Yeah, 17 years old.... a school party from Southampton."

"Vital statistics here."

"And telephone numbers!"

Robinson

There were dozens of flat slates by the side of the path. The messages were all dated the same day - last Saturday.

"OK, you can put your notebook away now," Roy called. "You're old enough to be their dad."

They continued down the track, leaving the messages for someone else to act upon, hopefully someone in the right age group.

It was about six o'clock when they walked into the picturesque village of Grange, now established as a regular stopping-point for walkers, with shop, postcards, refreshments and a telephone box.

Not least amongst the attractions is the unique double-arched bridge which spans the river and links the village with the main road to Keswick.

Half an hour later they were relieved to find the car was still there in the layby, and dissolved into the comfortable seats for a cat-nap before driving home.

"I still fancy another shot at Robinson," Roy remarked, "We should be able to get this walk down to about five miles."

"OK," replied Dave, "I'll go along with that."

So some weeks later they returned to Newlands, and parked by the church. They were aiming for a "horseshoe" walk, ascending by way of Hindscarth, and coming back down the ridge from Robinson.

The Hindscarth ridge was exhilarating, with views both sides, and a variation of terrain which included some interesting outcrops and a lofty path following the crest very closely.

They were surprised to see how quickly they gained the shoulder which connects the summits of the two mountains. Here they enjoyed wonderful views over the Buttermere valley, with the lake just peeping round the corner.

The summit of Robinson was only fifteen minutes away, and they found that the depression between the peaks was an ideal sheltered position to take lunch. There was no hurry - it was still only twelve o'clock.

The descent from Robinson took them onto a ridge route even more exciting than the last one. On the north side, glaciation and erosion had scooped huge slices out of the ridge, leaving a precipice, only six feet from where they walked.

Later, the path tumbled over craggy outcrops, and they found that on one particularly rough section the seat of their pants did more work than their boots. There was no real difficulty, and soon they were on the last grassy descent into the valley.

They were a little surprised to find that the complete route was not listed in any of the guide books, and although Wainwright had described both ridges in some detail, he never coupled them together into a circular walk.

"A pity really," Roy said afterwards. "It's a good walk, seven miles, quite easy, and I'd recommend it to anyone."

"Strange name for a mountain," Dave pondered. "Who was Robinson anyway?"

"Not sure," replied Roy, "but there is a reference in one of my books to a certain Mary Robinson from Buttermere. She was seduced by a local playboy about 90 years ago. Perhaps that's how it got it's name."

"And what did they call it before it became Robinson?"

ROBINSON FACTFILE

Robinson - 2417 ft.   Easy/moderate
Nearest towns - Keswick, Buttermere
Features - One of the finest high-level walks in England, including twin peaks Dale Head and Hindscarth
Choice of ridge routes into Newlands Valley

Snowdon

Snowdon, by the ridges! A tall order, but could it be done by a group of novices?

Members of the social club, operating from an office in the industrial West Riding of Yorkshire, were fairly conversant with hill-walking, and a hard-core of them made regular forays into the local scenery, looking for a bit of excitement through the weekends.

But there was always one special outing during the summer months, designed to offer more of a challenge, and this year Roy planned to introduce them to Snowdon. It had to be done by the scenic route of course, and there was only one which measured up to Roy's definition of a scenic route - the Crib Goch Ridge.

"I've done this with a party of school-kids," he told them. "There's nothing to worry about."

All the same, some of the regulars checked out the guide books for themselves, and the consensus of opinion was that they were letting themselves in for a tough one. One or two dropped out at that stage, having been put off by photographs of the ridge.

In the end, five regulars embarked on the journey which was to give them an experience they would remember for the rest of their walking days.

Based at Betws-y-Coed, they set up camp at one of the popular sites which seemed to offer all the facilities they needed. Saturday morning saw them crawling out of their tents at 5.30 am.

That in itself was a surprise, because they had been out the night before, celebrating their intended success. When Roy had suggested rising at 5.30, it was the beer talking!

Still, on reflection, it was not a bad time to start. The weather was good, the daylight long, and they looked forward to a full day's walking on the mountain.

Then they noticed the clouds building up. It hardly seemed fair, after weeks of hot, dry conditions, these were the first clouds they had seen.

"It's just the mountains," Roy explained. "You often get clouds forming on Snowdon, even on good days."

The six o'clock weather man confirmed it. Warm and sunny everywhere, with showers in the west. It still looked good.

They parked the cars at the top of the Llanberis Pass, and loaded their rucksacks. The clouds were still there, and a brief shower of large raindrops prompted them to include waterproofs, a good move, as it turned out.

There was no point in postponing the walk. The sun wasn't far away, behind that grey mantle of cloud, and there was every chance of it clearing up later.

By 8 o'clock they were walking up the "Pyg Track", a route well used by walkers, very rough but not dangerous. This track kept fairly well to the contours, heading for Snowdon summit, but keeping off the ridges.

The Crib Goch route, however, soon branched off to the right, immediately deteriorating into an indistinct chute of loose stone, marked occasionally by small cairns.

The summit ridge was somewhere up there in the mist, and as the clouds thickened it became difficult to pick out the cairned route amongst the outcrops of rock. It was beginning to rain, too.

"I don't like the look of it," Derek announced. Dennis and Barbara were looking apprehensive, and Jim was busy checking to see whether he had packed his waterproof cagoule.

"What do you want to do?" Roy asked.

"Carry on, I think," Dennis replied, ever hopeful.

"OK, here we go!" and Roy led the way up the line of cairns.

The cloud base was getting lower by the minute, and the valley was obscured by swirling mist. They were all cursing their luck, for what good it did, but they couldn't change anything, and the swearing only seemed to bring on the rain with added persistence.

Snowdon

There was no choice. Time for the waterproofs, and they hooded up against the elements before carrying on. This was not what they had expected.

The path was becoming very indistinct. The way had never been clearly defined, and they had been grateful for the line of cairns, but even these became fewer, and they spent much valuable time searching for them.

Eventually Roy had to abandon his attempts to find the path, and pressed on upwards, negotiating some rough scrambles over rocks that were becoming increasingly slippery in the rain.

"I think we should be more to the right," he shouted, hauling himself over a rocky shelf. "There are too many crags this way."

Progress was becoming more difficult. Each time they found a way around an outcrop they were confronted by another problem worse than the last. There were lines of huge rocks barring every attempt to climb, and it required all the ingenuity of Roy and Jim to get the party to safer ground. Each time they arrived on a new ledge they found new rock problems. To add to their predicament, the rain was coming down steadily and creating little waterfalls over the ledges.

"I don't like this," Barbara exclaimed. "Every time I get hold of a ledge I get a shoot of water up my arm. I'm wet through."

The higher they climbed, the more desperate they found the problems, but there was no choice but to continue, hanging on, heaving up and over, sometimes trying two or three routes before finding one which would go.

Roy found his long reach very useful, but that was no good to Barbara, who was much shorter by about twelve inches, and hadn't a chance of straddling a wide crevice. The greasy surfaces were deadly. They could not afford to let anybody slip, especially when the rocks below were so rough and sharp.

"Look!" shouted Dennis, pointing to his left. "An army unit!"

There were about six men, all clad in combat gear, climbing a course which looked even steeper and rougher than the one Roy was leading. They appeared to know what they were doing, but Roy would not be fooled into following them.

"They're off line," he said. "I still think the correct route is over there." He waved his arm to the right, where he thought the rocks looked smaller.

At every opportunity, Roy moved in that direction. Sure enough the rocks became less severe, and the footing less hazardous.

"The cairns!" shouted Dennis. "We're back on course!"

It was still tough. The slope seemed to get more severe the higher they climbed, but suddenly it levelled out, and a small pile of rocks indicated to them that they had reached the top - Crib Goch summit. As they peered over the cairn a strong wind hit them, threatening to blow them back again.

"That's the hardest bit done," Roy announced. "We're at three thousand feet now."

His voice was hardly heard in the wind, his words whisked away as he spoke.

"Can't see a thing," Derek complained. "My photographs aren't going to be worth much."

Jim looked around him as he clung on desperately against the gale.

"Where's the ridge?" he enquired.

Roy pointed into the mist. "Over there!"

Suddenly they were able to see the start of it. In the billowing fog it seemed to rock and sway, and kept disappearing as thicker cloud intervened. In some ways it was less awesome than it would normally have appeared. The poor visibility had completely destroyed the sensation of height. The 2000-foot precipice on each side was lost, and all they could see was a range of fifty feet or so. It looked very ordinary.

"Less hazardous than the climbing we've just done," Roy assured them. "No ledges or waterfalls!" Hitching up his rucksack, he led the way onto the first section.

"OK, as long as the wind doesn't blow us away," said Barbara, hanging onto Dennis's anorak bottom as she spoke.

The rain lashed them horizontally with renewed vigour, and water was beginning to find its way into any loose bits of clothing. The day was not cold, but the wind and rain were making it feel very uncomfortable.

They looked nervously over the north side of the ridge, but could only see a short way down the rock face.

It was a crumb of comfort for the ones who didn't like heights.

The air coming up from the valley had a fresh feel to it, and Dennis retreated from the edge. "There's a hell of a lot of empty space down there," he exclaimed.

"How about a happy photograph?" quipped Derek, reaching for his camera.

So, selecting a prominent rock, the party gathered around it, clinging onto each other, not knowing whether to try and smile, or to put on a miserable weather-beaten expression more fitting to the occasion.

Moving on again, they crouched low against the wind, crawling on hands and feet across the ridge, one rock at a time.

After a few minutes Roy paused. He had spotted a lone climber some distance behind them, catching up rapidly.

"Saw him earlier this morning," Dennis observed. "I spoke to him. He was coming up by the cairns."

As the young man arrived on the scene, he stopped to compare routes, relieved to find that he was on the right course.

"I followed those army recruits," he explained. "I thought they knew where they were going, so I tagged in behind."

"Where are they?" Roy asked.

"They got lost," the climber went on. "It was getting desperate. The sergeant just kept going, higher and higher, until you really needed ropes.

"We came to this horrible overhang, and he fell off. Fell onto some rocks and rolled about thirty feet, over some crags. We spent half an hour tying his leg up, all bruised and cut. They've gone back down now."

The young climber had then retraced his steps and found the cairns again.

"Want to join us?" invited Roy, and he nodded, grateful for some company.

Half an hour later, they noticed that the knife-edged path had become a good track, and they were no longer on the edge of a precipice. It was a bit of an anticlimax to realise that Crib Goch was behind them, and they hadn`t been able to fully appreciate the spectacle of the ridge. Now it was just plain uphill walking to the summit.

Coffee was taken in a small hollow behind a group of rocks, where the rain came straight down instead of across. Sitting on wet rocks had the effect of squeezing water out of the bottom of the anorak, and trickles of warm rainwater ran down their legs.

It was about midday when they reached the last peak before the Snowdon summit. From there it was only a short walk to the point where the mountain railway came up from the other side.

As they plodded up the track, one of the steam engines chugged into view, belching black smoke, pulling its single carriage up the steep gradient. Derek was surprised to see that it was full of tourists, despite the bad weather.

"It's always full," Roy remarked. "Some days you can't get on at all."

The train disappeared into a small siding where it began to disgorge its passengers, and Roy led his party past the station building, up to the large cairn which marked the highest point.

"Snowdon Summit, 3560 feet," he announced.

Then he noticed the others had already set off for the cafe which adjoins the station.

Inside the big double doors, crowds of walkers were gathered, just delighted to get in out of the weather. The first feel of the warm, humid air was a blessed relief. It signalled the end of a four-hour ordeal against the wind and rain, and they stood there for a couple of minutes allowing the water to drain off their cagoules onto the floor.

The walls were festooned with scores of anoraks, cagoules and capes, in bright yellows, orange, red and blue, all dripping water into an ever-increasing puddle.

Inside the cafe it was packed to capacity. The air was thick with steam as everyone sat round the tables drying out, drinking bowls of soup and pots of hot tea.

There wasn't a spare seat to be seen anywhere, and when one eventually became vacant, there was a puddle of water in it - water which had drained out of the occupant's shirt and trousers.

But all good things have to come to an end, and after a blissful half hour, it was time to gather up their rucksacks and put on the anoraks again.

Snowdon

There is something about a cold, wet anorak which lingers in the memory for its sheer cruelty. The feel of cold waterproofs going on top of a wet steaming shirt is not one to savour. It tends to send shivers running down the spine.

Derek's anorak was the worst, one of those old canvas ones which pulled over his head. It was still wet, thick and heavy, and water ran out of the pockets as he picked it up.

It had always been difficult to put on at the best of times, and simply impossible when full of rainwater. It took three of his companions to pull it down over his head, and he just stood there in a state of shock as the ice-cold water began to get through to his skin again.

The ultimate in cruelty and discomfort!

Pausing for a few seconds at the big double doors, they summoned up courage, and stepped out into the driving rain once more. The torture started again.

Below the rim of the ridge the weather didn't feel so bad. The wind dropped, and as they reached the lake at the foot of the mountain it actually stopped raining altogether. What a relief!

Back at the camp site the sun was shining and the ground was dry. A butterfly winged its way leisurely from one flower to another, and fellow-campers were building up their suntan on inflatable beds.

It was a different world.

SNOWDON FACTFILE

Snowdon, height 3560 ft. Heart of the Snowdonia National Park, only ten miles from the North Wales coast and the Island of Anglesey.

Snowdon is the highest mountain South of the Scottish border.

The **Snowdon** circular walk from Pen-y-pas, 1169 ft, on the Llanberis Pass visits the summits of Crib Goch 3023 ft, Crib-y-ddysal 3493 ft, Snowdon 3560 ft, Y Lliwedd 2947 ft, and the enclosed lake, Llyn Llydaw.
Moderate/difficult

The **Snowdon** Mountain Railway, built in 1896, is Britain's highest railway, and our only *rack and pinion* track.
The railway is 4½ miles long. Starts at Llanberis, 353 ft, and rises to Snowdon Summit Station at 3493 ft, with its well-stocked cafe and bar.

The Rakes

"What's a Rake?" asked Jeff.

"Well, it's a sort of..... it's a gully, a way up the mountain."

"I've looked in the dictionary," Jeff went on, "and it's not very helpful. Apparently it's a garden implement, used for raking the vegetable plot."

Further examination of the dictionary revealed, once again, the nautical reference to "incline from the perpendicular," but nothing specific about mountains, or the ways to get up them.

Then Roy produced a small collection of guide books, well-thumbed, and stuffed with a variety of bookmarks.

"I've managed to find some good ones," he announced. "Two in particular, on Scafell and Pavey Ark."

Both of them looked interesting, two mountains, each with a famous Rake.

Scafell was the higher of the two, overlooking Wasdale. The summit was reached by way of a steep gully, Lord's Rake.

Then on Pavey Ark, there was Jack's Rake, which looked more difficult, and this was to be found just above the Dungeon Ghyll Hotel in Langdale.

The guide books made many references to these "Rakes", describing them variously as a passage, a gully, a channel, a cutting, a ladder, a breach, and a groove.

"We'll do both of them!" Roy announced, and Jeff, surprisingly, agreed to the suggestion. Perhaps he didn't realise what he was letting himself in for. As it turned out, they were about to embark on one of the most rewarding of all their escapades, the unforgettable experience of the Rakes.

Scafell was to be the first.

From Wasdale Head there appeared to be two distinct choices of route. The easy one ran up the right hand flank, which was grassy but steep. Over to the left, between the two peaks of Scafell and Scafell Pike, the only logical approach led straight up Lord's Rake.

"That's the one we need," Roy explained, having studied the book. "We look for Lord's Rake just below the ridge."

Setting off in bright sunshine, they found the ascent very hard work, gaining height on a steep grassy tongue between two small streams. The crags around the summit were in view all the time, which had the advantage of encouraging them to greater efforts.

As Roy and Jeff toiled in the humid atmosphere, the crags seemed to move further away, a phenomenon well known to mountaineers. Sometimes it feels that you're never going to get there.

The last thousand feet were tortuous. Long rivers of scree ran down from the rocks above, making each step a supreme effort. If Roy and Jeff stood still for too long, the scree started to move and they were carried down along with all the other debris.

After half an hour of cursing and swearing they reached an outcrop which raised its head out of the scree, giving them a platform where they could rest for a few minutes and get out the coffee.

Above them was the ridge, a col between the two peaks, identified in the book as Mickledore. At first sight it looked like an easy passage between the two mountains, but Roy pointed out the towering block of black rocks just over to the right.

"That's Scafell Crag," he said. "It blocks the direct route onto Scafell summit."

Then Jeff spotted what they had been looking for. About 300 feet above them, he picked out a large vertical crack in the rocks.

"Lord's Rake!" he announced.

Sure enough, it was Lord's Rake, but there was an enormous wedge of loose scree which had to be negotiated first, and this was set at a ridiculously steep angle.

The Rakes

More scree! Jeff was already complaining after the last one, but clearly wasn't going to be put off.

On this tilted terrain, large boulders could never find a grip, and had long since disappeared into the valley below. Only the small stones remained, a loose mixture which crumbled and ran away at the touch of a boot.

Several rests later, they arrived at the entrance to the Rake itself.

Looking up, they could see the dark passage which separated the two halves of the crag. It was as though the whole mountain had split, leaving a rough stairway in between, climbing up at a steep angle towards a narrow col at the far end. The col itself appeared as a beacon of bright light at the end of a dismal passage.

"It's like looking up the cellar steps," Jeff remarked.

"Steps?" Roy replied. "There's nothing to put your foot on."

It was soon evident that there were not going to be any steps at all, just a desperate slope of greasy rock and loose pebbles. The Rake was smooth and dead straight, as if cut by mechanical tools.

Starting as an uncomfortable scramble, it became more difficult as the walls narrowed, and the floor became steeper and steeper. Eventually the loose pebbles underfoot gave way to damp polished rock, where the steepness made it impossible for stones to lie.

The enclosing rocks, the dampness, the silence, and the sound of their own breathing all combined to make it an eerie, lonely place, where all outside influences were shut out.

There were holds on both sides, small and polished on the left, but very loose on the right. The loose ones looked like bits of old slate, which came away very easily with the pressure of a hand. Roy found it easier to straddle the passage as much as possible, taking some of the weight off the hands. Looking down between his legs he could see the slope of the floor disappearing steeply towards the bottom of the Rake, an alarming sight which made him cling on desperately. It was not a place to be careless.

Going down would be delightfully simple, just one long slide that would probably take the seat out of your pants. Going up, though, was working against the forces of nature and gravity.

Roy struggled, panting, grunting, cursing, and paused occasionally, spreadeagled, to think out the next move. More toe-holds, finger-holds, friction holds and straddles, then another piece of rock would come away, leaving him hanging on with one hand, scraping with his foot to find something which would take his weight.

Jeff had extra problems. His legs were shorter, and he was faced with finding his own route, whilst dodging the loose stones coming down from Roy's efforts.

Suddenly Roy found "jugs" on his left, good clean holds which helped to get him over the final section. Two more minutes, arriving at the col, he collapsed, panting, against the rock wall.

"That was the hardest hundred yards I've ever done," he gasped.

Jeff hoisted himself onto the shoulder alongside him, and they stayed for a couple of minutes enjoying the spectacle of the craggy formations which surrounded them. It was a truly wonderful position, in the middle of the most impressive rock landscape in England.

From the col, the airy path descended a little, then up to another small col, followed by a short slippery scramble onto a third. This was the final one, which opened up a clear scramble to Scafell summit. They had made it!

"One thing's for sure," Roy said. "It's the only way up from that side, without ropes, that is."

They briefly discussed the possibility of going down the same way, but rejected it in favour of the grassy slope offered by the west flank. This route took them on an uncomplicated descent to Wasdale Head, where the barman at the local Inn was pleased to provide much needed refreshments.

A perfect end to a rewarding day!

"What about Jack's Rake?" Roy ventured, not knowing what Jeff would think after the first day's experiences.

"Yes, OK," Jeff nodded. "Tomorrow?"

So it was all arranged, and the following morning they were climbing the grassy valley alongside the bouncing stream which flows near the Dungeon Ghyll Hotel in Langdale.

The Rakes

Jack's Rake was going to be a completely different proposition from the tortuous treadmill of the previous day, and Roy was well aware of the difficulties it might pose.

He had surveyed the crags of Pavey Ark many times from a safe distance, whilst sitting on the shore of Stickle Tarn. The entire rock face plunges vertically down, almost into the waters of the tarn itself, in a continuous unbroken cliff. It appears to be completely inaccessible, except for rock climbers armed with pitons and ropes.

True, there are grassy flanks to either side, offering a safe passage to the top, but these routes lacked the challenge, the threat and the exposure of the direct assault.

After looking carefully at the rock face for some time, he detected a trace of a fault line running from the bottom right, up to the top left. It was the only obvious break in an otherwise impregnable fortress of stone - Jack's Rake! The guide book recommended caution.

Could it be done? Was it feasible? There was only one way to find out.

They skirted the shores of the tarn until they reached a position just below the start of the Rake.

From here they could clearly see the cleft in the rock, and for the first time they were able to understand how Jack's Rake happened to be there.

It was an obvious fault line, where a slice of the mountain had split away from the main crag, leaving a groove. This was partly filled with loose rock, creating a kind of rough stairway, and the outer rim of stone formed a natural parapet between the footway and the empty space below.

As Roy led up the first section, he was pleased to find it fairly easy, with plenty of good holds for both hands and feet. Also, there was little sense of exposure or danger, thanks to the parapet on the lower side.

Jeff was also finding it very easy. He had no rock-climbing experience, but that didn't seem to worry him. He just threw himself into it with all the exuberance of youth, keeping a couple of yards behind Roy.

As the climb progressed, the friendly parapet was always there, giving complete reassurance, and they were able to enjoy the privilege of being on a sheer rock face without the fear of falling off.

There were occasional problems where the holds became rather sparse, but these could be overcome fairly easily with some delicate footwork, climbing the top of the parapet in preference to the gully. These were really traumatic moments, and for a few anxious steps they were poised precariously over the face of the crag. Then, having overcome the difficult bits, they returned to the safety of the groove.

They knew it would be difficult in parts. After all, it was not a stairway - you don't find many natural stairways in the mountains, and there were many sections where it needed a hefty pull with the hands to help bring the boot up to a high ledge.

"We're about half-way," Roy called to Jeff. "From here it's easier to carry on than to go back."

Jeff had never even thought of going back. The Rake had been fairly friendly so far. "None of that desperate slogging," he observed.

Then Roy found a large grassy terrace, a flat area where they could safely unpack their rucksacks and get out the cameras for a dramatic photograph or two. Just the place for coffee!

"Not too difficult," Jeff remarked. "I've climbed worse places when I've been out hiking." A bit of an understatement, perhaps, but in all honesty there had been no real problems.

It was not a time to become complacent, however, and a few minutes later they were negotiating some very lofty ledges.

It was a very exhilarating place, and commanded splendid views over Stickle Tarn and the Langdale Valley. They could also pick out the distant gleam of Lake Windermere.

The sense of exposure was getting critical. There was no longer a parapet to protect them, and they frequently looked straight down from the ledges to the tarn at the foot of the crag.

Another grassy terrace appeared, a welcome relief from the heart-stopping traverses of the last half hour, but their joy was short-lived as the track arrived at an obstructing buttress.

The next few steps were perhaps the most hazardous of the whole climb.

The Rakes

The path, sparse as it was, disappeared completely, to be replaced by a rock shelf not much wider than the sole of a boot. It was firm, level, and safe, but the dizzy drop down the face of the buttress was something else!

The last few feet of the traverse were a nightmare. The thin ledge dwindled to nothing, and the bulge of the buttress seemed to offer no holds at all. A small grassy shelf across the gully looked very doubtful, and the consequences of slipping were obvious, but Roy didn't even pause to think about it. With one almighty stride, he leaped across.

A few seconds later, Jeff followed. "Easy!" he grinned. "What's next?"

From there it was only a hop and a skip to the top of the Rake, and soon they were sitting by the small cairn admiring the view. Below the crag, a group of walkers could be seen taking lunch on the banks of Stickle Tarn. Were they contemplating climbing Jack`s Rake?

"Great walk!" Jeff remarked. "But a bit airy in places."

Roy grinned. "Next time I need a Rake," he commented, "I'll get one from the garden shed!"

THE RAKES FACTFILE

Lord's Rake -
A passage between the summits of Scafell Pike, 3210 ft. and Scafell, 3162 ft.
The two highest summits in England.
Lord's Rake is 100 yards long, strenuous but not dangerous.
Approaches - By road from Whitehaven, Ravenglass to Wasdale Head,
        longer approaches on foot from Borrowdale or Langdale.
Overlooks Wasdale.

Jack's Rake -
A cleft, or fault line running obliquely up the face of Pavey Ark, 2288 ft.
Jack's Rake is 225 yards long, tricky in places, dangerous in bad weather.
Overlooks Great Langdale.
Nearest town - Ambleside.

Eagle Crag

There are many references to "Eagle Crag" in the various guide books. In common with "Raven", "Heron", "Jackdaw" and "Crow", the name signifies the beautiful age-old tradition of living alongside Nature in these wild and unspoilt places.

Amongst the selection of "Bird" crags, everyone has his or her particular favourite, one which conjours up memories of exciting walks, nail-biting climbs, or simply the joy of wandering over the fell-tops during a peaceful holiday.

For Roy and Jeff, it was purely by accident that they happened to be in Borrowdale at the right time. It was by sheer chance that they were looking for a camp site where they could pitch their tent before dark. It was even luckier to have found Stonethwaite, a gem of a valley, a green paradise in the shade of a friendly, lofty crag - Eagle Crag.

From the village of Stonethwaite, a track runs for a quarter of a mile over a bed of large stones which passes for a road, but once over that obstacle the scene is one of peace, tranquility, privacy and complete freedom from the traffic of the 20th century. The valley is idyllic, the camp site perfect for a week of isolation from all the little irritations of life.

The choice of walking is endless. Most walks start and finish at the camp site. Low level routes include field and forest, bridleways, rock pools, streams, waterfalls, village paths and farm tracks. The fells which surround the valley are reached within a few minutes, and include Greenup Edge and the Langdales, Dock Tarn and Watendlath, Bessyboot and Eagle Crag.

Jeff and Roy were impressed. They lost no time erecting the tent as near as possible to the small river, which babbled over a bed of pebbles and boulders. Its constant tinkling and rushing sound quickly lulled them off to sleep.

Breakfast was taken in the warmth of the early morning sun, as it broke over the rim of Greenup Edge, rising like a red orb. Hues of orange and yellow painted the mists which lingered on the steep faces of Eagle Crag. Silence reigned over the scene, except for the distant call of a chaffinch, and the gurgle of water flowing softly over the rocks.

It was a great temptation to sit back, relax, and simply let the day go by, but Roy had other ideas. He had studied the face of Eagle Crag and was beginning to get ideas about climbing it.

The more he thought about it, the more excited he became.

"Looks quite straightforward in the book," he announced, and Jeff leaned over to have a look.

"A bit airy," he observed, "but there's definitely a way up, if you can find it."

It was easy to examine the crag from the camp site. All the main features stood out quite clearly in the sunlight.

At first it appeared daunting, impregnable, a buttress of inaccessible rock, but as they studied the formations, they could trace the successive layers of rock and the small grassy shelves which separated them. Small breaks in the continuous lines of crags gave a clue to the route, where gullies provided a rough stairway onto the next shelf.

"It's worth a try," Roy suggested, and Jeff agreed.

A few minutes later they were walking up the valley, heading for the bracken-covered slope at the foot of the climb.

The path was almost non-existent in the deep fronds of bracken, shoulder-high in places, but eventually this gave way to tufted grass. This, too, disappeared, as they reached the steep scree below the crag, and soon they were searching the first layer of rocks for the start of the ascent.

Eagle Crag

It was very important that they should begin at the right place. The crags were precipitous, except for one line of weakness, and this point could not be seen from below. Roy thought they would find the small gully after about half an hour's climbing.

A faint track led them towards an overhanging buttress, and here the path became more distinct. "Someone's been here before," Jeff observed. "This must be the right way."

"Looks good to me," Roy replied, and launched himself into the first slippery scramble onto a grassy ledge.

Following the base of the next outcrop, they found themselves on a narrow green tongue, and five minutes later a small stony gully led upwards onto another ledge.

"So far so good," shouted Roy, and Jeff joined him, hardly panting.

"Time for a coffee?"

"Yes, did you bring it?"

"No."

"Neither did I."

"Right, we'll manage without."

After that completely useless bit of conversation, they searched their pockets and found some mints and a few liquorice sweets, which seemed to fill the emptiness, and continued upwards.

Having achieved another higher terrace, they stood for a while admiring the views all around. The camp site seemed miles away, and beyond Stonethwaite the Borrowdale valley could be seen, dappled in shades of green.

Their lofty position was getting critical, and they clung on tightly, very conscious of the sheer drop as the ground fell away from their feet on three sides.

A bank of rocky crags on the right looked awesome, very perpendicular, and extended for some distance up towards the clouds. The rocks on the left were very similar, and it became very obvious that the only possible way up was by way of the narrow groove they were climbing.

It was a very privileged position, looking across the face of the cliff. About twenty feet away, a pair of jackdaws were sitting on a small ledge observing the intruders, calling to each other in a tone which Roy said was either alarm or defiance - he couldn't decide which.

Either way, the birds were quite safe. Even with the aid of ropes, he felt that the towering precipice was beyond his capabilities, and why should he want to disturb them anyway?

"It's like sitting on a window ledge fifteen floors up," he murmured. "I've often wondered what it takes to clean windows on tower blocks."

Jeff grimaced. "Yeah, you can count me out."

As he spoke, he was easing himself around a small rocky outcrop onto a ledge, trying to ignore the chasm below him. Roy followed his lead, and soon they were on a wide grassy shelf, looking for the next move.

In front of them the rocks were split by several small fissures. Most of the gaps were upright, and filled with loose stone, much too hazardous for the likes of Roy and Jeff. They explored to the right, scrambling over some low outcrops, until they saw a much wider break.

This seemed to be the one they had been looking for. It was firm enough to clamber up without dislodging any rock, and soon they were standing on another grassy tongue leading up obliquely towards the top of the crag.

"It's less steep now," Roy called back to Jeff. "I think we're nearly there."

He was right. After a couple of minutes they found a small cairn perched on a flat rock - the summit of Eagle Crag.

"I haven't seen any eagles," Roy remarked.

"I don't think we're likely to," Jeff replied. "There aren't many around these days."

They spent a few minutes savouring their position, trying to identify the various mountain tops which surrounded them.

Ahead of them they were relieved to see the simple undulations of a broad fell-top, a choice of easy ways off the mountain. It was a choice which they were very pleased to make, after the nerve-shattering ledges of the direct route.

Roy led the way down into Langstrath, the adjacent valley, to examine Blackmoss Pot, where the river falls into a deep pool. It proved to be well worth the journey,

Eagle Crag

especially as there was a fair torrent of water coming over the waterfall.

The pool was deep, dark and sinister, set in a long, deep gorge with vertical sides. There were many places where Roy and Jeff could walk round, admire and photograph the scene. The stillness of the water was a complete escape from the trauma of the climb.

Roy sat on a rock near the pool, gazing up at Eagle Crag, the dominant summit overlooking the valley.

"Look - Eagles!" He pointed skywards at two silhouettes floating round the upper crags.

Jeff watched them for a minute. "Jackdaws," he announced.

"They're not jackdaws," Roy retorted, "but they might be buzzards. The shape is more like a buzzard, but they don't normally fly so high. They should be over fields and woods."

"So they're not buzzards then...." Jeff thought for a while. "And I don't think they're jackdaws either. They're too big, and they glide too much."

The silhouette, the glide, the size - it all seemed to add up to a rare sighting of the Golden Eagle, but Roy and Jeff still remained unconvinced. If only they had been more experienced in bird-spotting, they might have made a more positive identification.

Jeff marked it in his diary as a "possible sighting."

Back at camp, they spent a happy hour trying to construct stepping stones over the stream, but gave up in the end. The current took all the rocks away.

As darkness fell, they strolled through to the village, looking for some entertainment. Then, on the stroke of midnight, they took a long, varied route back to camp, through fields at the edge of the open moor.

"What a beautiful Summer's night," Roy remarked.

"Yes, how about a walk over the moor," Jeff suggested.

"In darkness?"

"Yes, come on," Jeff enthused, slipping through the gate and almost falling over a sleeping sheep.

It was difficult to see anything at all in the blackness, and the landrover tracks they were following quickly disappeared, leaving them to fall over tufts of grass, and stumble into wet hollows.

Half an hour passed as they felt their way through the scrubby grass. The silence was unbearable. Silhouettes of trees began to take on ghostly forms in the inky darkness, and a large grey rock suddenly got up and walked away. It turned out to be a rather untidy sheep.

There were more sheep on the moor, surprised to see figures looming up out of the gloom, and retreated, as sheep usually do.

"Can't see a thing," Jeff remarked, feeling with his feet for a suspected hollow.

They stood listening to the retreating sheep. All they could hear was the sound of "Dump-a-dump-a-dump" as they thundered past, and the "Pat-pat-pat" of a lamb close behind.

Then there was the "Phutt-Phutt-Phutt" as a large bird took off from almost under-foot, causing Roy to collapse with a suspected heart attack.

"Phutt-Phutt", then a shrill "Hike-Hike!" somewhere to the right, and another "Hike!" to the left. Then silence.

They almost rolled down an unseen hillside, and a large mound, which looked like a grassy hillock, rose up and moved away....."Dump-a-Dump-a-Dump-a-Dump".... "Pat-pat-pat".... and another "Hike-Hike!"

" Phutt-Phutt-Phutt!"

" Phutt-Phutt!"

" Hike!"

" Help!"

Stumbling back towards the track, they felt like intruders in a world which belonged to the wild things, but it was an experience unlike anything else. It was unreal.

What a relief to find the camp site, their cosy tent, and something resembling normality. The babbling of the nearby river soon settled their nerves, and lulled them into a deep sleep.

There was a tremendous downpour before dawn. Thunderstorms rolled over the hills, and the sound of water drumming on the canvas of the tent was ear-splitting, drowning out all other sounds, including speech.

Water began flooding into the cooking extension, and there were anxious moments when droplets started to dribble down the tent-pole. Roy thought they had sprung a leak, but then he remembered there was a seal missing from the top of the pole.

Eagle Crag

As daylight transformed the scene, the sky turned from grey to a pale pastel blue, streaked with ribbons of cloud. The storms had gone.

All around the camp site, lakes of water had gathered, and there were some quite lively torrents where previously they had seen only dry gullies.

Then Jeff noticed the small river which had been so friendly and clear. It was flowing deep, fast and dark grey as it raced between its banks, almost spilling over into the field.

"We'd better get out of here!" he shouted.

Roy hadn't even emerged from his sleeping bag, but after peeping through the flap and seeing the rising water, he dressed in a sudden flurry, and helped Jeff to dismantle the cooking gear and pack the bedding into the car.

"Did we have to pitch in the lowest point we could find?" Roy moaned. "We should have known better."

"Yes, but it looked great down by the stream," Jeff reminded him. "We didn't think it would come up like this."

As the tents were stowed away, they saw the water beginning to creep over the banks onto the camp site.

It was an undignified departure from such an idyllic spot. Several other tents, pitched sensibly on higher ground, remained safe and dry.

Those lucky campers would undoubtedly enjoy another day of sunshine.

And some great walking!

EAGLE CRAG FACTFILE

Eagle Crag - 1650 ft.   Part of Sergeant's Crag, 1873 ft.
Ascent - Difficult, especially in bad weather.
Descent - Dangerous, route indistinct over crags.

Eagle Crag overlooks Stonethwaite Valley,
an idyllic green valley off Borrowdale near Rossthwaite.

Nearest town - Keswick

Barf

Roy and Jeff began looking at Barf as a half-day walk, a relaxing finish to a busy week.

They had viewed this little gem of a mountain from the safe distance of the public bar at the Swan Hotel. There was a time when the main Cockermouth road ran straight past the building, and travellers would see the hotel as they sped through to Keswick, often calling in for some refreshment to break their journey.

Nowadays, the reconstructed Cockermouth road is a fast dual carriageway a short distance to the east of its original course, leaving the Swan to enjoy an idyllic existence in a quiet backwater. Luckily the purity of the ale was never affected by the traffic, or lack of it, and the hotel has become, to some of us, more of a special evening out.

The mountain of Barf, overlooking the Swan, looked an easy proposition, being only 1500 feet high, similar to Loughrigg and Helm Crag, but only half the height of nearby Skiddaw.

The gradient, however, was steep, so steep that rocks and grass simply rolled off its slopes, and trees had been unable to gain a foothold.

One solitary object stood, like a sentry, immune from the effects of gravity. Perched on a rock shelf half-way up the scree, gleaming white like a beacon, was the Bishop, a grotesquely shaped rock which seemed to stand guard over the mountain, at the same time keeping an eye on the public house below.

The Bishop was freshly painted in brilliant white, making it stand out from the dull grey of the surrounding slate. It caught the rays of the morning sun and seemed to shine so brightly it might have been a light source in its own right.

In the guide book there were references to men carrying buckets of whitewash up the hill from the Swan, but judging by the difficult scree slope, Roy thought it much more likely that whoever renewed the paint would take the easy way, and use a sealed can of emulsion from the local supermarket.

Jeff looked up from the map, a smile on his face. "I'd like to meet the chap who dreamed up this mad story."

"You might be waiting a long time," Roy replied. "I think he's dead!"

He was sure in his own mind that the tradition of the Bishop went back a long way, but search as he might in all the walking books he couldn't find any reference to its history.

"We'll have to make our own history," he announced. "We'll go and have a look this afternoon and see what all the excitement is about."

At two o'clock they began their exploration in the woods which clothe the lower section of the climb.

Here in a small clearing was an upright rock, about as tall as Roy, but slender and bent like an old man. This was the "Clerk", also referred to in the book, again without explanation as to its origin, or its purpose.

"There could be a connection," Jeff suggested. "The word *clerical* would make him a clergyman, so he might be related to the Bishop."

"Good thinking!" Roy leaned against the rock and opened a can of orange.

"You've only just just started, and you're drinking already."

"Saves me from carrying it up there," Roy explained.

There was some logic in the argument, as they soon discovered when they left the Clerk to embark on the toughest section.

There was loose scree everywhere. It even ran down into the trees, making it difficult to make upward progress even before they had left the shelter of the wood. At least they were able to use the tree branches to heave themselves along, a luxury which they knew would disappear once they reached the steep section.

Barf

After only a few yards the trees gave way to a barren landscape of rock and shale, a scene of desolation which seemed to carry on as far as the eye could see. The slope was just about as severe as any walk could be. Any steeper and they would have needed ropes!

Jeff led off, his boots sinking well into the soft surface.

"It's OK," he announced. "Not as loose as I expected."

There was a sudden flurry of stones and Jeff found himself prostrate on the floor against Roy's feet. He again launched himself onto the shale and managed only six feet before sliding down almost to the point where he started.

Then he swung round a tree as a small avalanche of rock cascaded from above.

Roy hadn't moved, yet he was already three yards in front of Jeff. "You'd be better walking backwards!" he suggested.

With commendable effort, Jeff clawed his way back to where Roy stood, and tried a completely new approach to the steep slope. This time he trod carefully on the scree, taking great care not to move anything as he went. It seemed to work.

A few minutes later, they were making good progress up the hillside, making deep footprints in the shale, aiming obliquely across the slope to lessen the disturbance.

There were no trees, no grass and no bracken on that barren hillside, only a scattering of gorse bushes some way to the right, where the terrain looked to be more solid. Some distance above them they could see towering rock faces, and rocky ledges where mountain ash and oak had taken hold and made safe roosting perches for the crows.

Meanwhile, half-way up the scree, Roy and Jeff stopped for a minute, legs splayed across the surface, panting for breath. It was hard work. They discovered that no matter how carefully they placed their feet, they still slid downwards with every step.

Roy was busy picking up bits of rock and scrutinising the markings. One piece was particularly well patterned.

"This is fossilised wood," he announced, tossing it over to Jeff, who wasn't really interested anyway, and the action of avoiding the rock made him slide a couple of feet further down.

"Here's another - a bigger one," Roy shouted, seizing a piece of fossil weighing a few pounds. "I'm taking this."

The piece of rock protruded from the top of his rucksack, making him feel top-heavy, just at a time when he would have appreciated less weight rather than more.

It wasn't getting any easier, but at least they could see the white rock of the Bishop not far above, and this spurred them on to greater efforts.

The surface was so unstable that on occasions they found themselves sliding slowly downwards, and were forced into a series of rapid steps to recover the yards they had lost. The flurry of activity had the effect of dislodging further quantities of stone, and they had to wait until the avalanche stopped before climbing again.

Eventually they reached the platform of rock which supported the Bishop, and were relieved to find solid ground amongst bracken and tufted grass. It was a delightful spot, a comfortable seat looking down over the Bishop towards the Swan Hotel, some 700 feet below.

The Bishop was a very solid-looking figure, somewhat grotesque in its uneven shape, but very nobly standing guard over the valley. It was hard to estimate its height, but it was at least twice the size of the Clerk.

"Looks a bit like a chess piece to me," Roy suggested. "An oversized version of a bishop. Do you think that's how it got its name?"

"Could be... but then on the other hand, maybe not."

Its white coat gleamed brightly in the sun, giving it a rather special importance, the kind of importance that a lighthouse might command, standing on the cliff-tops over a dangerous sea.

It was easy to see why the Hotel had adopted this rock. There were very few features on the mountain worthy of preservation, yet this proud sentry stood out above the scree like some super-human form.

It was the Hotel's own special rock, a mascot which would draw in the crowds from miles around.

"I can see it all," Jeff announced. "Listen to this!"

As he spoke, he placed one foot on the platform, and waved his hand towards the Hotel.

"This is how it all started..........

Barf

"It must have been about a hundred years ago, when the locals used to get paid on a Friday and come to the public bar to spend it all on beer."

"Nothing much has changed," ventured Roy.

"Except there was no tele'," Jeff pointed out. "And the local pub was the centre of attraction in those days.

"And I suppose there was a local Bishop?" Roy mentioned this, prompting for some more ideas on its origin.

"I don't think so," Jeff went on. "I imagine that's a more recent name. There's a Bishop in Bath, and a few comedians in Keswick, so I think they got together and called this one the Bishop of Barf!"

"I still think it looks like a chess piece," said Roy. "And what about the paint?"

"I'm just coming to that," Jeff continued. "It was just about closing time, on a good Summer's evening, middle of June. Some of the chaps were a bit fed up with playing darts.... looking for something to impress the women.

"One of the chaps had a brilliant idea, a bit of a competition. We'll go and paint that rock. We have two teams, each man carries a bucket of whitewash and a brush, and we race up and paint it before closing time. The last team back pays for the beer!"

"And what if someone spills all the whitewash?" Roy asked.

"He has to go all the way down and collect another bucket."

"That's brilliant," Roy laughed. "We'll ask the landlord to organise it tonight!"

Feeling very much refreshed, Roy and Jeff recorded the scene with a couple of photographs, and continued up the rough tracks leading towards the summit.

It was interesting walking, scrambling up gullies and traversing rock barriers, then there was a false summit before the true one came into view. It was all so much easier than the scree had been.

On reaching the cairn they saw what the book had been telling them, that this mountain was not a separate peak, but merely a shoulder of a higher hill, Lords Seat.

However they looked at Lords Seat, it was an anticlimax. The beauty, the enjoyment, the challenge and the success were all behind them, on the slopes of Barf.

Ahead of them they saw a change in the scenery, mass forestation. It was still pleasant in its own way, offering a cool, shady walk on good tracks, but nothing could match the magic of Barf!

BARF   FACTFILE

Barf - 1536 ft.   Moderate
Part of Lord's Seat, 1811 ft.

Nearest towns - Keswick, Cockermouth.
Features - The Bishop, The Clerk.
Overlooks Bassenthwaite Lake.

Great Gable

Roy and Jeff had saved the big one for the end of the holiday. Great Gable, they knew, was not the highest of the Lakeland fells, but the prospect of the infamous Napes Ridge and the much-photographed Needle made it a rather special climb. This was a connoisseur's walk, an expedition which had everything, from hiking, to scrambling, and ultimately to rock-climbing.

The day was sunny and calm, and the small fleecy clouds flitting across a deep blue sky gave the mountain scenery a touch of friendliness which seemed to promise that nothing would go wrong today.

There were two obvious approaches to Great Gable, one of them slightly longer than the other. The shorter one started at Wasdale Head, over on the western side, but as their base was in Keswick, this would entail a 40-mile drive over the mountain passes, an exercise which would have to be repeated in reverse at the end of the day.

"The Borrowdale approach is the pretty way," Roy explained, "but the walk is about five miles longer. How do you feel?"

"I'm OK," Jeff assured him. "How about you? You've passed the big five-O now!"

"Don't worry, I've got my crutches," Roy grunted in reply. "And there's no hurry, we've got all day."

Packing plenty of liquid refreshments, sugary cakes and fruit, they drove to Seathwaite, at the far end of Borrowdale, and began walking at about 10.30. The timing was deliberate, because they were able to have coffee and scones before leaving the car, saving them a few pounds of extra weight in their rucksacks.

Within half an hour they arrived at Stockley Bridge, a picturesque arch of stone which spans the tumbling waters of the Gill.

This is a photographer's paradise. The bridge is constructed over a series of small falls, where the water enters a wide pool, then babbles down a rocky ravine, and continues down to Borrowdale as a lively stream. They paused for a few photographs before heading uphill fairly steeply.

As the path levelled out, Styhead Tarn appeared in a broad valley, its smooth surface reflecting the summer sky like a mirror. Just to the right was the mass of Great Gable, and they saw the brown eroded track reaching up the flank of the mountain towards the summit. It looked a tough one, suggesting that the hardest part of the walk was still to come.

"A bit steep!" Jeff decided.

"Don't worry, that's not our path," Roy said, a reassuring smile on his face. "It's the Napes Ridge we want, and that's round the other side, just below the summit ridge."

"Then the fun starts!" Jeff reminded him. "I saw it in the book. It's a really desperate scramble up the last bit."

Roy grinned again, which seemed to confirm Jeff's remark, and he followed apprehensively as Roy searched for the right path.

The track around the mountain was very indistinct, nothing like the well-beaten brown paths they were used to. It was more like a scree traverse, with occasional level stretches between long tracts of loose stone.

Soon a group of rocks appeared ahead, and they noticed a couple of rock-climbers half-way up the side of the tallest buttress.

As Roy and Jeff drew level, they paused and watched the leader negotiating a thin crack, which appeared to be his only means of support.

Roy called up to the nearest, hoping the surprise wouldn't cause him to fall off.

"Is this the right way to the Napes?"

"Sure is!" came the reply. "This is Kern Knotts."

"Thanks - Take care!"

Great Gable

The path slanted upwards across easy scree, which at that point had been worn level by the action of boots over the years. Soon a line of high crags appeared against the sky about five hundred feet above them.

"I guess that's the Napes Ridge," Jeff exclaimed. "I can't climb that!"

It certainly appeared formidable. Towers of naked stone reached towards the sky, hundreds of feet of inaccessible rock.

"We don't climb the direct route," Roy assured him. "There's an easy gully at the far end."

"How easy is Easy?" Jeff asked. "I know your easy gullies... We'll probably be hanging by our finger tips before we've finished!"

"Not quite," Roy laughed. Jeff gave him a look of disbelief.

The path led them below the first group of tall rocks, then turned across a steep scree chute called "Great Hell Gate."

It was a dramatic feature, a stone-filled gap in the ridge where avalanches rolled down on their way to the valley, two thousand feet below.

The scree turned out to be fairly easy, and there was no evidence of any recent rock-slides. Jeff felt happier. It was going to be a piece of cake after all.

The next group of rocks was very much bigger than the first, taller, steeper and more impressive. They knew from their research that they would find the famous "Needle" amongst this formation, and this spurred them on to greater efforts.

They negotiated several awkward buttresses, aiming to maintain the same height as they contoured across the face of the ridge.

"That's it," Jeff exclaimed, pointing to a buttress slightly above them. "The Needle!"

It was indeed the Needle, protruding from the base of a naked cliff, a slim tower of clean rock narrowing to a fine point. It was so smooth, it appeared to be polished, especially the slight overhang a few feet below the top. It was an awesome prospect.

"There's no way I'm going to climb that," Roy decided. "I'd need a top-rope." Jeff agreed.

With more effort, and much grunting and puffing, they climbed the gully at the side of the Needle, and wedged themselves between some rocks for a few minutes rest and - guess what - another cup of coffee.

"We're in the *Dress Circle*," Roy explained, looking at the guide book. "This is supposed to be the viewing area for watching the climbers."

To describe the *Dress Circle*, one has to imagine a wide, vertical cleft in the face of the mountain, and the walker has to find a series of airy steps taking him into the cleft, around the back and out again. It's all quite exposed, with lots of space above and below, and the final corner emerging from the cleft is an awkward stride around a protruding rock.

"Thank goodness for that!" Jeff exclaimed, as they safely regained solid ground and continued across the rocks. The Needle was soon well behind them and out of sight.

"What's next?" Jeff enquired. "Sphinx Rock?"

"Yes," affirmed Roy. "I think we'll go down a bit and take the easier path below."

It was safer and much less exposed on the lower path. Here, a much-used track leads around the mountain, avoiding the most arduous sections, but those who choose to follow it invariably miss the main features of the ridge.

Roy and Jeff soon realised that the path was too low, and that if they walked too far along it, they would not see Sphinx Rock at all. The next twenty minutes were spent strenuously regaining height, trying to find the gully which would lead them back on course.

Sphinx Rock eventually appeared on the skyline above them, but the silhouette was not the one they had expected. It looked more like a cat from their lowly vantage point.

"Cat Rock!" Jeff exclaimed. "The other name for it. In the book - it all depends where you are when you see it. From here it's a cat, and it turns into a sphinx when you get up to it."

Amazing! As they drew level with the rock, the tail became an ear, and the feline shape turned into a rocky head resembling a Red-Indian totem pole.

"Not much like a sphinx," Jeff remarked.

"But what a view he's got," Roy observed.

Great Gable

The scenery was unparallelled, fields, trees and lakes. The green valley of Wasdale contrasted sharply with the grey rocks of Gable. Wastwater sparkled warmly in the sun, and some way beyond, the gleam of clean sands on the Cumbrian coast gave way to a pale blue sea on the distant horizon.

"If ever I was turned to stone," Roy thought, "I'd be Sphinx Rock!"

It was a fitting end to a great traverse. There had been many interesting features along the way, and now it was time to find their way off the ridge, onto the summit.

It was not going to be easy.

Just around the corner, the steep ascent of Little Hell Gate was another of those desperate scree chutes, but Roy thought he could climb straight up the ridge from the Sphinx. "Easier than all that loose stuff," he said.

"After you," Jeff insisted, and Roy began the ascent of a steep groove, looking for hand-holds in the jagged rock on each side.

"It's nearly vertical," he reported back to Jeff. "Stand by to catch me!"

"You'd be better without your stick," Jeff called.

Yes, his walking stick was definitely getting in the way. Very good on rough tracks and moorland, but useless on steep rock. Wedging himself across the gully, Roy threw it up the face of the rock, hoping it would catch on something. After several attempts the stick lodged in a crack, and he climbed up after it.

On the final section, Roy broke out in a cold sweat as he realised the precarious position they were in.

There was no margin for error.

"I thought you said it was easy!" Jeff challenged.

"Not too bad...."

"All right for you..... legs like a spider. Why did you choose a rock climb?"

"I didn't."

"Well, what do you call this?"

"Don't blame me, I didn't know."

It had developed into a moderate rock climb, and they were a hundred feet up, without ropes.

Eventually they hauled themselves onto the level top of the ridge and laughed loudly with relief. From there it was only a hop, skip and a jump to the summit of Great Gable, and five minutes later they were congratulating each other around the cairn.

Great Gable is only fifty feet shorter than some of the famous peaks in the Scafell group, but always looks more impressive because of its unique shape. Its vertical sides fall away dramatically in every direction.... a true peak in its own right, standing in isolation above the surrounding valleys.

Seen from Wasdale, its craggy western face dominates the head of the valley. From Borrowdale the peak appears even taller than Scafell, and walkers approaching from Langdale or Honister experience the same illusion.

It is easy to imagine why Great Gable has been given such a proud name. This is a proud mountain, a mountain worthy of every accolade. To Roy and Jeff it was a memorable climax to a successful expedition.

GREAT GABLE FACTFILE

Great Gable - 2949 ft.   Moderate/difficult

Nearest Towns - Keswick, Ravenglass
Nearest approach - Wasdale Head
Features - Napes Needle, Sphinx Rock, also known as Cat Rock
High level Gable traverse
Ascent from Borrowdale passes Styhead Tarn.

Reflections

There is something about mountains that is difficult to explain. What is it that forms the attraction, and why are so many men and women so completely addicted to mountain walking?

For me it all begins when I head towards Kendal and catch my first sight of the hills. Arriving in Windermere, I begin to pick out the features that I know - Helvelyn, the Langdales and Loughrigg. It's magic. All seem to beckon to me, to invite me in a silent but persuasive language of their own. It's a message that makes the heart beat faster, and the feet twitch with an expectancy known only to those who have been captured by the magic.

The visual beauty of the Lakes is not hard to understand - the rolling fells, the rugged crags, the placid lakes, bouncing streams, and stone-built houses with blue slate roofs all combine to present a panorama of exciting prospects.

Embarking on the first walk of the week brings the realisation of numerous challenges that face the walker. The ability to climb, to walk and to sustain effort over a long period, on a variety of terrains and gradients is a factor which makes this pastime unique.

In every person lies a natural, sometimes hidden desire to extend. Walkers must often raise their efforts in moments of extreme exhaustion and emerge better beings at the end of the day.

The use of proper equipment and clothing provides a safety margin, but nothing can take away the satisfaction of personal achievement in terms of effort, whether the objective is a short ascent of Loughrigg or a strenuous climb on Scafell.

Good equipment and clothing are essential in the battle against the elements. A warm summer's day offers pleasurable walking whatever the objective, but a wild day of gales, heavy rain or snow creates a situation of confrontation, against everything that the mountains can throw at us. It is a battle that must be won, and even a pair of wet feet and a soaking vest cannot detract from that ultimate, special enjoyment of sitting in the bar or cafe by an open fire, glass in hand, having come through the storm unscathed.

So it's all a challenge, and to win is to enjoy. But that's not the whole story. There is also the mental attitude, which varies from one man, or woman, to another, and is far more difficult to explain. It is a very subtle science which everyone experiences in their own way.

Walking is an escape from the little irritations of life. The average walker is often alone, over long periods of time. A problem in the mind can either be reasoned out at leisure, or cast aside, to be replaced by soothing thoughts of mountains, photography, the next lunch stop, or merely the hypnotic trance created by the rhythmic tread of boots on gravel.

Companionship is another important aspect of mental and physical relaxation. Parties large or small achieve the satisfactions of mind and body as a group effort. To discuss the events of the day over a glass of what-you-fancy is just one of the enjoyments.

Even the lone walker will often find companionship, for every man and woman met on the fells will pass the time of day, stop for a chat, or exchange information. This unique attitude has grown to be a tradition in the mountains, whilst in a city centre you would never dream of talking to everyone you see!

In many ways, lone walkers experience their own personal feelings for the hills. In their isolation, they sense that the mountains communicate with them more intimately, a feeling which can become very real.

Of course safety margins must be broader, confidence in one's own ability and a thorough knowledge of the challenges are essential.

Reflections

Employing our own talents against the mountain takes us far into the unknown parts of the scenery, also into the unknown parts of the mind. We live, we feel, we become different beings, and most of all, we become part of the mountain, small insignificant specks on the side of a vast peak, mere dots in the infinity of Nature. Where else could we be as one with the environment, with the elements, and with our inner selves?

Over the years I have developed an interest in painting the landscapes which hold so much fascination for me. Back at the old grammar school, art was presented in such rigid form, and there was never the opportunity to develop what I call "free" painting. It was only in later years that I was able to experiment with watercolours and try to emulate the well-known Lakeland painters.

Art is such an indefinable science, I shall probably never know whether I have fully succeeded in projecting the images as I saw them. How can you judge, when every painter develops a different style? How can a Constable be compared with a Cooper?

Now, as the years pass, the legs ain't what they used to be. The heart is always there, but there is the constant reminder, the realisation that youth never returns. In its place, there is a deeper understanding, a more intimate love for the mountains.

Two books, "My Mountains" and "Mountain High" bring to life all that I have loved over the years. There is achievement, immense enjoyment, companionship, comedy and some sadness, but most of all there is the kind of adventure which many a city-dweller will enjoy and understand, and situations which the average walker will meet any day of the year.

We all experience a deep-rooted respect for the countryside, and I sincerely hope that others will continue to visit the mountains, enjoy them, and preserve them.

May future generations derive the same pleasure from walking in the hills, and may we always find peace and tranquility in the wide open spaces.

Book 1, **MY MOUNTAINS**, *available from many bookshops, completes the collection of mountain memories..........*

Bowfell	*a dangerous route*
Coniston Old Man	*caught in a storm*
The Joys of Youth	*the comedy of youth organisations*
The Langdale Pikes	*lost in the bogs*
Snowdon	*successful youth expedition*
Rock Climbing	*introduction to rock climbing*
The Screes of Honister	*a fatal attraction*
Climbing in Cumbria	*just how good are we?*
Dunnerdale	*even in defeat, there is humour*
Scafell Pike	*in fog, rain and snow*
Ben Nevis	*midsummer's day madness*

Published by *WAKEWALKER* **Books January 1994**

Index

Ambleside	15,16,33,43, 53,56,72	Eagle Crag	32,45,51,52 73-76
Arrochar	35,37	Eagles	51,75
Bampton	40	Easedale Tarn	54,55,56
Barf	46,77-79	Eel Crags	63
Bassenthwaite	79	Elter Water	15
Ben Arthur	13,35-37	Emley Moor	58
Ben Lomond	36	Ennerdale	52
Ben Nevis	8,84	Fairfield	34
Bessyboot	73	Fort William	35
Betws-y-Coed	42,65	Grange	29,64
Bishop of Barf	46,77-79	Grasmere	11,19,33,34, 53-56
Blackmoss Pot	74	Great Gable	47,48,80-82
Blease Fell	22,24	Great Hell Gate	81
Blencathra	10,20-24	Greenup Edge	73
Borrowdale	26,29,32,48, 49,72,73,74, 76,80,82	Grisedale	17,18
		Hall's Fell	20,21,23,24
Bowfell	84	Haweswater	38-41
Braithwaite	49	Heatwave	53-56
Bridge House	43	Helm Crag	11,12,33,34, 77
Burtness Comb	51,52		
Buttermere	14,49-52,56, 62,63,64	Helvelyn	9,17-19,21, 34,83
Castle Rigg	10,24	High Spy	62,63
Catbells	21,62	High Stile	14,49,51,56
Cat Rock	81,82	Hindscarth	26,27,44,52, 62-64
Causey Pike	21,49		
Clerk, the	77-79	Holmfirth	61
Cobbler, the	13,35-37	Holme Moss	25,57-61
Cockermouth	56,77,79	Honister Crag/Pass	8,49,56,62, 82,84
Codale Tarn	55,56		
Coniston Old Man	8,84	Huddersfield	61
Copper Mines	26,63	Inveraray	37
Crag Hill	50	Jack's Rake	30,69-72
Crib Goch	65-68	Kendal	83
Crib-y-ddysal	68	Kern Knotts	80
Crummock Water	49,56	Keswick	20,24,33,49, 62,64,76,77, 79,80,82
Dale Head	52,62,63,64		
Derbyshire	57		
Derwent Water	62	Knowe Crags	23
Dock Tarn	73	Langdale	15,30,69,71, 72,73,82-84
Doddick Gill	21		
Dress Circle	81	Langstrath	74
Dungeon Ghyll	69,70	Lanty's Tarn	17
Dunnerdale	84	Lion and the Lamb	12,33,34

Index

Little Hell Gate	82	Scafell Pike	28,49,69,72,84
Llanberis	65,68	Scar Crag	50
Llyn Llydaw	68	Sergeant Man	54-56
Loch Lomond	35	Sergeant's Crag	76
Loch Long	35	Seathwaite	80
Lord's Rake	28,69-72	Shap	40
Lord's Seat	79	Sharp Edge	21,22,24
Loughrigg	16,31,53,54,56,77,83	Sheepbone Rake	51
Maiden Moor	62	Skiddaw	21,77
Mardale	38-41	Slate Quarries	26
Mickledore	69	Snow	22-24,57-61
Napes Needle	47,80-82	Snowdon	42,65-68,84
Napes Ridge	80-82	Snowdon Railway	67,68
Narrow Edge	21	Solicitors, the	52
Newlands	27,63,64	Sourmilk Gill	54
Patterdale	17,19	Sphinx Rock	81,82
Pavey Ark	30,69-72	Steeple	52
Pennines	57,61	Stickle Tarn	71,72
Penrith	20	Stockley Bridge	48,80
Pen-y-pas	68	Stone Circle	10,24
Pillar	52	Stonethwaite	32,45,73,74,76
Pyg Track	65		
Rakes, the	69-72	Striding Edge	9,17-19,51
Red Tarn	17,18,19	Styhead Tarn	80,82
Rest and be Thankful Pass	35,37	Swirral Edge	19
Robinson	26,27,44,49,52,56,62-64	Threlkeld	20,22,24
		Ullswater	17,38,39
Rock Climbing	84	Wasdale	69,70,72,80,82
Rossthwaite	76		
Saddleback	21,24	Watendlath	73
Scales Tarn	21	Waterhead	16
Scafell	8,21,28,69-72,83	Whiteless Pike	49,56
		Windermere	38,71,83
Scafell Crag	69	Y Lliwedd	68